Praise for
For Women Only

"Shaunti's signature message, which she has shared around the world with millions of listeners, is life changing and something every woman needs to hear. Every time I have given someone this book, I have seen lives and marriages changed!"

—LYSA TERKEURST, *New York Times* best-selling author
of *Made to Crave*

"This one short little book brings a long-lasting, big impact on marriage—which is why I've been taking groups of women through a *For Women Only* study every year since I first read it. Shaunti's message has impacted my relationships personally, and I've seen some amazing transformation in the lives and marriages of others."

—HOLLY FURTICK, lead pastor's wife, Elevation Church,
Charlotte, North Carolina

"What an important book!"

—BETH MOORE, Bible teacher, best-selling author
of *So Long, Insecurity*

"In our weekly couples' study, we read and discussed both *For Women Only* and *For Men Only* over the course of several months. They were fascinating and very helpful. The findings in these books about how men and women think are so enlightening. My wife and I think these books should be required premarital reading!"

—Comedian JEFF FOXWORTHY

"You're about to gain some fresh insight into some of the mysteries of masculinity. *For Women Only* is a book that I believe will provide understanding and bring harmony to a lot of marriages."

—Bob Lepine, cohost of *FamilyLife Today*

"Ready for an eyeopener? Shaunti Feldhahn has uncovered a mountain of meaningful information for any woman wanting to understand men at a profound level."

—Drs. Les and Leslie Parrott, Seattle Pacific University;
authors of *Love Talk*

"Men are in agreement on this one: *For Women Only* is one book every husband wishes his wife would read! It's a practical, thought-provoking message that will show you what you should do—and not do—when it comes to your relationship with the man in your life. Read it, and you're bound to have many 'aha!' moments that could revolutionize your relationship."

—Valorie Burton, best-selling author of *Successful Women Think Differently* and *What's Really Holding You Back?*

"*For Women Only* is the best book I have read for women, about men. Shaunti's research, facts, and stories in this little book create an incredible read for all women. Single, married, divorced, or not even allowed to date yet should all read this and come to understand the key truths that will help in your relationship with any man. I bought a copy, read it, was astonished, and then bought ten more and sent them to everyone on our team."

—Craig Gross, founder of XXXchurch.com

"This book is a treasure box that never seems empty of wisdom. Every time I dig in, my hands and heart emerge filled with tools that help me know myself better and relate to the people I love more effectively. If you've already read it, you should read it again. And if you are just opening these pages for the first time, buckle a seat belt over your soul and get ready for a ride you won't soon forget."

—PRISCILLA SHIRER, best-selling author of *One in a Million*

"We gave this book to every woman in our congregation for a special event. I interviewed Shaunti during all our worship services. The response was incredible. She has an engaging, compelling way of presenting her findings about how men think. It helped open the eyes of women to the real needs of the men in their lives, and it gave men a common language to talk with their wives. I urge churches and other groups to give her the opportunity to share this message."

—ANDY STANLEY, author of *Enemies of the Heart;* senior pastor, North Point Community Church, Alpharetta, Georgia

Praise for
For Men Only and *For Women Only*

"Whenever Shaunti Feldhahn appears as a guest on our radio program, we know that listener response will be enthusiastic. She has a way of connecting with the audience that is unique and compelling. We're thankful for the unique perspective she provides not only to the Christian community but to the culture at large."

—JIM DALY, president of Focus on the Family

"These are the books I pass out to people as the best on the subject. Shaunti Feldhahn has the rare ability to do impeccable research and then make her findings incredibly practical. There is something to learn on every page."

—JIM BURNS, PhD, president of HomeWord; author
of *Creating an Intimate Marriage*

"Whatever Shaunti Feldhahn researches, read. Actually, do more than read: study! Her ability to ask the right questions, find the right answers, and communicate the results clearly and practically sets her apart as a gifted researcher. Her content guides and changes lives."

—EMERSON EGGERICHS, PhD, best-selling author
of *Love and Respect*

"Shaunti Feldhahn has a unique gift for helping men understand women, and women, men. Her books are the best I know at providing rich and practical gender understanding that can be used immediately. I highly recommend both all the time!"

—ROBERT LEWIS, author of *Raising a Modern-Day Knight;*
founder of Men's Fraternity

"Shaunti Feldhahn has the unique gift of communicating a Christian worldview in a language everyone, Christian or secular, understands. Her experience and educational background qualify her to speak and write authoritatively about relationships and how people respond. I personally have seen and felt the impact of her research. She is the go-to person for our organization when we need insight."

—PHIL WALDREP, founder, Women of Joy conferences
and Phil Waldrep Ministries, Decatur, Alabama

Shaunti Feldhahn

What You Need to Know About the Inner Lives of Men

REVISED AND UPDATED EDITION

MULTNOMAH
BOOKS

For Women Only

Scripture quotations are taken from the following versions: The Holy Bible, English Standard Version, copyright © 2001 by Crossway Bibles, a division of Good News Publishers. Used by permission. All rights reserved. King James Version. The Holy Bible, New International Version®, NIV®. Copyright © 1973, 1978, 1984 by Biblica Inc.™ Used by permission of Zondervan. All rights reserved worldwide. www.zondervan.com. The Holy Bible, New Living Translation, copyright © 1996. Used by permission of Tyndale House Publishers Inc., Carol Stream, Illinois 60188. All rights reserved.

Details in some anecdotes and stories have been changed to protect the identities of the persons involved.

Hardcover ISBN 978-1-60142-444-0
eBook ISBN 978-1-60142-210-1

Copyright © 2004, 2013 by Veritas Enterprises Inc.

Cover design by Mark D. Ford

Published in association with the literary agency of Calvin Edwards, 1220 Austin Glen Drive, Atlanta, GA 30338.

Published in the United States by Multnomah, an imprint of the Crown Publishing Group, a division of Penguin Random House LLC, New York.

Multnomah® and its mountain colophon are registered trademarks of Penguin Random House LLC.

Library of Congress Cataloging-in-Publication Data
Feldhahn, Shaunti Christine.
    For women only : what you need to know about the inner lives of men / Shaunti Feldhahn. — Revised and Updated Edition.
        pages cm
    Includes bibliographical references.
    ISBN 978-1-60142-444-0 — ISBN 978-1-60142-210-1 (electronic)
    1. Man-woman relationships—Religious aspects—Christianity. 2. Man-woman relationships. 3. Men—Psychology. 4. Marriage—Religious aspects—Christianity. 5. Marriage. I. Title.
    BT708.5.F455 2013
    248.8'435—dc23

                                                          2012044949

Printed in the United States of America
2018—Revised Edition

10

Special Sales
Most Multnomah books are available at special quantity discounts when purchased in bulk by corporations, organizations, and special-interest groups. Custom imprinting or excerpting can also be done to fit special needs. For information, please e-mail specialmarketscms@penguinrandomhouse.com or call 1-800-603-7051.

For Jeff.
My beloved, my friend.

SONG OF SOLOMON 5:16

Contents

One

LIGHT BULB ON!

How I Woke Up to What I Didn't Know About Men

The other half of the people on the planet already know what you're going to read in this book.

As newlyweds, my husband and I lived in Manhattan, and like all New Yorkers, we walked everywhere. But I quickly noticed something strange. Quite often we'd be strolling hand in hand and Jeff would abruptly jerk his head up and away. We'd be watching in-line skaters in Central Park or waiting to cross the street in a crowd, and he would suddenly stare at the sky. I started to wonder, *Is something going on at the tops of these buildings?*

Turns out, something *was* going on, but it wasn't up in the buildings.

Have you ever been totally confused by something the man in your life has said or done? Looking at your boyfriend's rapidly departing back, have you ever wondered, *Why did that make him so angry?* Have you ever been perplexed by your husband's defensiveness when you asked him to stop working so much? Yeah? Me too.

But now, after interviewing and surveying thousands of men, I can tell you that the answers to those and dozens of other common perplexities are all related to what is going on in your man's inner life. Most are things he wishes you knew but doesn't know how to tell you. In many cases, they're things he has no idea you don't know. This book will share those interviews and those answers. But be careful. You might be slapping your forehead a lot!

> I can tell you that the answers to dozens of common perplexities are related to what is going on in your man's inner life.

HOW IT ALL STARTED

Let me tell you how I got here. It all started with the research for my second novel, *The Lights of Tenth Street.* One of my main characters was a devoted husband and father. Because I had to put thoughts in his head, but had no idea what a guy would be thinking in a given situation, I interviewed my husband, Jeff, and many other male friends and colleagues. ("What would you be thinking if you were the character in this scene?") It took me a while to figure out how to handle what I found.

You see, in many cases, what I heard stunned me. Not just because what the men were thinking was so surprising but because it was so foundational. These weren't feelings that popped up every few months but were deep fundamental needs, fears, doubts, and thought patterns that occur in men every single day. It didn't matter whether the man I was talking to was old or young; what his racial or cultural background was; whether he was married or single, a churchgoer or an atheist, a corporate executive or a factory line worker—I kept hearing similar things.

For example, the character in my novel was a good guy who loved his wife and kids, was a devoted churchgoer and godly man, and a successful businessman. But he struggled with his thought life, especially the visual temptations that beckoned from every corner, from the secret traps of the Internet to the overt appeal of the miniskirt walking down the street. So, in short—and this is what shocked me—I discovered that instead of being unusual, my character was like almost every man on the planet. Including the faithful husbands I was interviewing.

That revelation led to a host of others, and following those trails led me to the thousands of personal and written interviews with men—including several professional, nationally representative surveys—that form the core of this book. I interviewed close friends over dinner and strangers in the grocery store, married fathers at church and the single student sitting next to me on the airplane. I talked to CEOs, attorneys, pastors, technology geeks, business managers, the security guard at Costco, and the guys behind the counter at Starbucks. I even interviewed a professional opera singer, a household-name movie star, and a former NFL offensive tackle with a Super Bowl ring. No one was safe.

Light Bulb On!

As I learned about what was going on at their secret inner core, I discovered that there were many things I thought I understood about men—but really didn't. Once I got below the surface, everything changed. I felt like a cartoon character who suddenly had a light bulb over my head.

Even better, it turned out that those revelations were mostly about things that my own husband always wished I knew but that he couldn't figure out how to explain. And that was a common refrain from most of the men I talked to. Although I still make many mistakes in my relationship with my husband—and will continue to—finally grasping these things has helped me to better appreciate and support him in the way that he needs.

> These revelations were mostly things that my own husband always wished I knew but that he couldn't figure out how to explain.

And I'm not alone.

This is the second edition of this book, which originally came out in 2004. If I was surprised at these revelations about men, it was nothing to how surprised and grateful I was to see how much this message helped so many other women, men, and marriages! My team and I were flooded with thousands of e-mails from women and men sharing how simple "aha moments" had changed everything. Divorces had been canceled. Relationships were restored. How couples understood each other was changing—all because suddenly they knew one or two things they hadn't known before. This research was talked about on hundreds of media outlets and rapidly went all over the world. *For Women Only* sold more than a million copies in twenty-two different languages, precisely because these truths about men are so important and so universal.

In response to requests, Jeff and I researched and wrote the companion project, *For Men Only: A Straightforward Guide to the Inner Lives of Women,* which came out a few years later. Eventually we followed that one up with a few others in the "Only" series.

Over the last few years, we've been amazed and humbled to

see the sheer reach and impact of this research on so many women, men, teens, and families. And it all started because of a few simple, surprising, research-based truths that are updated and expanded for the second edition.

For this new edition, I have incorporated several new elements, including research I've done and new surprises I've uncovered since the original book released, as well as some key truths learned by brain scientists in recent years that often help explain why men think the way they do. I have even added an entirely new chapter—"The Thinker"—which unwraps a truth about men that I was so perplexed by before but found to be life changing once I understood what was going on. I hope you find all these "light bulb *on*!" moments to be life changing for you as well.

Why Was This Surprising?

When all this started, I and countless women I talked to were surprised to be so…surprised. Why? I think it's because we women assume we already know plenty about a man's inner life. But that may be one of our problems. Most men *know* they are confused about women. But because we don't tend to feel as confused about them, we can go for years without knowing what we don't know.

Let me give you an example. We have all heard that men are visual, but what exactly does that mean?

> We all know, for example, that men are
> visual, but what exactly does that mean?

It turns out that what that means *in practice* is the key thing—the specific insight that can help each of us be a better wife, girlfriend, or mother. The difference is vast between having the vague notion that men are visual and knowing that the sexy commercial that just flashed across the screen might become a mental time bomb that explodes on him the next day. Or, on a different topic, the difference is vast between helplessly wondering why something made him so upset and having the insight of thousands of men to help us understand not only what is going on but also how to prevent that problem from arising in the first place.

Actually, there was a kind of double surprise in this research. When I interviewed men and drew some conclusions, they would often say, "But women already know that. Surely they know *that.*" All too frequently I found myself replying, "Well, *I* didn't know that." Thousands of other women, I've learned, don't either. And since the same is true on the men's side, no wonder we have misunderstandings and conflict!

Yet the solution is often simple. Both Jeff and I have been astounded to discover that the majority of relationship problems do not stem from the big, intractable issues. Instead, they tend to spring from basic human cluelessness. From simple, avoidable misunderstandings. From a "light bulb *on!*" moment that never happened.

EIGHT REVELATIONS

So here are the revelations this book is going to deliver—eight insights that will take you from "surface level" to "in practice" in your relationships with a husband, boyfriend, or son.

As with us women, the inner life of a man comes as a package, with all these elements melded together and wrapped up inside. Every area affects every other area, and I'm only covering those few areas that I thought were the most important, surprising, and helpful.

Our Surface Understanding	What That Means in Practice
"Men need respect."	➡ Men would rather feel unloved than inadequate and disrespected.
"Men are insecure."	➡ Despite their "in control" exterior, men often feel like impostors and are insecure that their inadequacies will be discovered.
"Men avoid issues by 'checking out.'"	➡ Men address issues by first pulling away to process and think—so they can better talk about them later.

Our Surface Understanding	What That Means in Practice
"Men are providers."	→ Even if you personally made enough income to support the family's lifestyle, it would make no difference to the mental burden he feels to provide.
"Men want more sex."	→ Your sexual desire for your husband profoundly affects his sense of well-being and confidence in all areas of his life.
"Men are visual."	→ Even happily married men struggle with being pulled toward live and recollected images of other women.
"Men are unromantic."	→ Actually, most men enjoy romance (sometimes in different ways than women) and want to be romantic—but hesitate because they doubt they can succeed.
"Men care about appearance."	→ You don't need to be a size 3, but your man does need to see you making the effort to take care of yourself—and he will take on significant cost or inconvenience in order to support you.

THE SURVEYS

Although some of these revelations may be hard to believe, each has been repeatedly tested and carefully validated with highly reliable evidence—including, at last count, four groundbreaking professional, nationally representative surveys of more than sixteen hundred men. Two sets of experts have assisted me: Chuck Cowan at Analytic Focus, who is the former chief of survey design at the US Census Bureau, along with the survey team at the internationally respected firm, Decision Analyst. The surveys we developed together were meticulously planned and executed, and designed to deliver reliable results (the surveys had a 95 percent confidence level, ±3.5). In total, the anonymously surveyed men, ranging in age from twenty-one to seventy-five, answered several dozen questions about their lives and about how they think, what they feel, and what they need. The surveys stressed that we weren't dealing with outward behavior as much as with the inner thoughts and emotions that led to their behavior.

I also conducted multiple, more informal surveys, often to follow up with specific groups—for example, with a group of four hundred anonymous churchgoing men, and another of male business executives. Amazingly, across all these surveys there were very few differences.

After all the surveying, the results of my personal interviews were confirmed—when this whole thing started, I hadn't just happened to interview the weirdest men on the planet! Instead, all the anecdotes and quotes you will read in the pages ahead are backed up by statistically valid evidence.

BEFORE WE START: GROUND RULES

You're probably rarin' to turn the page. But first I'd like to offer some ground rules:

- If you're looking for male bashing or proof that your husband or boyfriend is indeed a cad, you won't find it here. I honor the men who shared their hearts with me, and I hope that by sharing their insight, more women might come to understand and appreciate the wonderful differences between us.

If you are looking for male bashing or proof that your husband is indeed a cad, you won't find it here.

- This book is not an equal treatment of male-female differences. Nor do I deal at all with how your man should relate to *you*. Yes, we women obviously also have needs, but since the theme is the inner lives of men and my space is limited, I'm focusing entirely on how women relate to men, not the other way around. (That is also why the personal-relationship surveys did not poll gay men.) You and your man can find the "other half of the story" in *For Men Only.* (That said, if you and your mate are reading both books, one great tip is to read the book about *you* first—in other words, he reads this book and you read *For Men Only.* Highlight and make notes in the margins about which points matter most to you. Then when you trade books, you are each reading a personalized copy.)

- Realize there are exceptions to every rule. When I say that "most men" appear to think a certain way, realize that "most" means exactly that—most, not all. You or your mate may actually find that you are more like the opposite sex in some areas. The key is to sincerely look for what matters most to *your* man.

- Some readers will be dealing with serious issues beyond the scope of this book. If you or the man in your life fall in that category, please get the experienced and specialized help you need. (You can also go to forwomenonlybook.com to explore more resources.) Fortunately, understanding these points about men can make for a helpful starting point on your road to healing.

- These findings reveal how men normally think and feel, not necessarily what is right behavior. You may find some insights distressing because they affect your view of the men in your life and your view of yourself. It would have been more comfortable for me to exclude certain statements, but I realized I was hearing things men often want us to understand but may not be willing or able to say directly to their spouses or girlfriends. Please realize that in most cases, these comments have little to do with *us*— they just reflect the way men are wired. And we should celebrate that fact. After all, it is because he is wired as a man that you love him.

- You'll notice a faith-based thread in these pages. Thousands of churches now require couples planning to get married to read this book and *For Men Only*. I also spend a lot of time speaking in the faith arena. That said, we surveyed men regardless of cultural background or religious belief, and my aim is for this book to be accessible and helpful to everyone.

> The more we understand the men in our lives, the better we can support and love them in the way they need to be loved.

Finally, and most important, I hope that this journey is not just about learning intriguing new secrets. The more we understand the men in our lives, the better we can support and love them in the way they need to be loved. In other words, this revelation is supposed to change and improve *us*. In the last ten years, I've seen that in almost every case, if we are willing to do that (even if it is one-sided at first), the other outcome we so deeply desire—a more satisfying relationship with the men we love—is sure to follow.

So read on, ladies, and join me as we journey into the fascinating inner lives of men.

Two

YOUR LOVE IS NOT ENOUGH

Why Your Respect Means More to Him than Even Your Affection

*Men would rather feel unloved
than inadequate and disrespected.*

When I was a year or two out of college, I went on a retreat that profoundly impacted my understanding of men. The theme of the retreat was "Relationships," which as you can imagine was of great interest to a group of single young adults. For the first session, the retreat speaker divided the room in half and placed the men on one side, women on the other.

"I'm going to ask you to choose between two bad things," he said. "If you had to choose, would you rather feel alone and unloved in the world *or* would you rather feel inadequate and disrespected by everyone?"

I remember thinking, *What kind of choice is that? Who would ever choose to feel unloved?*

The speaker then turned to the men's side of the room. "Okay, men. Who here would rather feel alone and unloved?"

A sea of hands went up, and a giant gasp rippled across the women's side of the room.

The speaker then asked which men would rather feel disrespected, and we women watched in bemusement as only a few men lifted their hands.

Then it was our turn to answer and the men's turn to be shocked when most of the women indicated that they'd rather feel inadequate than unloved.

> The speaker asked the men, "Who would rather feel unloved?" A sea of hands went up.

WHAT IT MEANS

While it may seem foreign to us, the male need for respect and affirmation, especially from his woman, is so hard-wired and so critical that *three out of four* men would rather feel unloved than disrespected or inadequate. In other words, if he had to choose, a man would give up feeling that his wife loved him, if he could just feel that she respected him! Look at the survey results:

Think about what these two negative experiences would be like: to feel alone and unloved in the world OR to feel inadequate and disrespected by everyone. If you were forced to choose one, which would you prefer? Would you rather feel...? (Choose one answer.)

Alone and Unloved		74%
Inadequate and Disrespected		26%

0%   50%   100%

When I originally tested the survey questions, I discovered that many men had a hard time answering the "unloved versus disrespected" question. Chuck Cowan, my survey-design expert, warned me that might happen. *But why?* I wondered. *Those are two totally different things!*

Then one of my readers tested my survey questions on ten men who didn't know me. When I got the surveys back, only one note was attached: "A lot of the guys fussed over question 3 [the question above]. They did not feel the choices were different."

Finally the light bulb came on: *A man equates the two. If he feels disrespected, he is going to feel unloved.* And what that translates to is this: if you want to love your man in the way he needs to be loved, then you need to ensure that he feels your respect most of all.

The funny thing is, most of us *do* respect the men in our lives. But too often, it turns out, our words or actions convey exactly the opposite—without our ever intending it! Have you ever been totally perplexed when a man responded negatively to something and wondered, *What did I say?* Me too. As it turns out, this issue is often why.

A Disrespect Barometer

So how do we know when we've crossed the disrespect line? Thankfully, there is one easy barometer: our men's anger.

Before I elaborate, let me ask you: If you are in a conflict with the man in your life, do you think it is legitimate to break down and cry? Most of us would probably answer yes. Now let me ask another question: In that same conflict, do you think it is legitimate for your man to get really angry? Many of us have a problem with that. We'd think he's not controlling himself or that he's behaving improperly.

But Dr. Emerson Eggerichs, author of the groundbreaking book *Love and Respect,* has an entirely different interpretation. He told me, "In a relationship conflict, crying is often a woman's response to feeling unloved, and anger is often a man's response to feeling disrespected."

"Anger is often a man's response to feeling disrespected."

If a man can't articulate his feelings in the heat of the moment, he won't necessarily blurt out something helpful like "You're disrespecting me!" But rest assured, if he's angry at something you've said or done and you don't understand the cause, there is a good chance that he is feeling the pain or humiliation of your disrespect.

If you want confirmation of this, consider the response from the survey. More than *80 percent* of men—four out of five—said that in a conflict they were likely to be feeling disrespected. Whereas we girls are far more likely to be wailing, "He doesn't love me!"

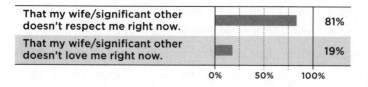

Even the best relationships sometimes have conflicts on day-to-day issues. In the middle of a conflict with my wife/significant other, I am more likely to be feeling... (Choose one answer.)*

That my wife/significant other doesn't respect me right now.	81%
That my wife/significant other doesn't love me right now.	19%

0%   50%   100%

"Unconditional Respect"

Just as you need the man in your life to love you unconditionally, even when you're not particularly lovable, your man needs you to demonstrate your respect for him regardless of whether he's meeting your expectations at the moment.

"We've become such a love-dominated culture," Dr. Eggerichs says. "Like the Beatles said, 'All you need is love.' So we've come to think that love should be unconditional. But respect must be earned. Instead, what men need is unconditional respect—to be respected for who they are [that is, our husbands], apart from how they do."

Notice that in chapter 5 of the letter the apostle Paul wrote to the church in the city of Ephesus—one of the most frequently cited Bible passages on marriage—he never tells the wife to love her husband. And he never tells the husband to respect his wife (presumably because we already tend to give what we want to receive). Instead, in different ways, the passage repeatedly urges the husband to *love* his wife and the wife to *respect* her husband.

Often, we women will naturally say "I love you" but at the same time want to control things. Unfortunately, men tend to interpret this as disrespect and distrust (which it sometimes is). But marriage invites all of us to place the other person's needs above our own (he's required to do that too, remember), and it does tremendous things for your man to know that you are choosing to respect him—in other words, choosing to trust, appreciate, admire, believe in, and honor him.

It's a Choice!

And that reveals the most important aspect of demonstrating respect: It is a choice. A choice that we make out of reverence for God and love for our husbands. Just as our men can choose to demonstrate love toward us even if they don't feel it at the moment, so we can and should demonstrate respect toward them.

> Just as our men can choose to demonstrate love toward us even if they don't feel it at the moment, so we can and should choose to demonstrate respect.

What, then, is the woman to do who no longer respects the man in her life? While my surveys have found that this affects a relatively small percentage of marriages, there are certainly real issues out there. As a place to start, I encourage you to consider two factors that seem related:

First, you may be caught in what Eggerichs dubs the Crazy Cycle—the unfortunate dynamic where your man doesn't give enough love, so you don't give enough respect, so he feels slighted and doesn't give enough love…and on and on. Your choice to respect can break that cycle.

And second, feelings often follow words or actions, rather than the other way around. For example, if you regularly disparage your husband to him or to your friends, don't be surprised if you feel contempt. But your choice to show him respect can change your feelings. In fact, your choice to show respect can transform your entire relationship. I have seen and heard of thousands of lives and relationships changed by just such a one-sided choice.

IT'S NOT REAL
UNLESS YOU SHOW IT

Which brings us to what respecting a man looks like in practice. You wouldn't believe the number of men who told me that they do recognize, deep down, that their mates respect, value, and appreciate them…but the problem is that their wives don't necessarily show it outwardly—or even know how.

Want to know what respecting your husband but not showing it feels like to him? Well, consider that awful joke: "Why do I have to tell my wife I love her? I told her that when we got married!" Just as a wife feels dreadful if her husband never expresses his love, so a husband feels dreadful if a wife never demonstrates her respect. To him, it's the very stuff of love and it's not negotiable.

Of course, the way he needs to feel your respect is quite different from the way you need to feel his love. Most women appreciate it when a husband says, "I love you." But, as I discovered pretty quickly, it just doesn't do it for a guy to hear his wife coo, "Oh, honey, I respect you *so* much." He *does* need to hear, "Honey, I'm so proud of you" and "I trust you" and "Thank you for what you did." But demonstrating through your day-to-day actions that you do truly respect him often means even more than words.

> The way a man needs to feel your respect is quite different from the way you need to feel his love.

The surveys came back with some practical insights on how we can do just that. Men's comments revealed six key needs.

Need 1: Respect His Judgment

The men were really touchy about this. A man deeply needs the woman in his life to respect his knowledge, opinions, and decisions—what I would call his judgment. No one wanted a silent wallflower (nor would I advocate becoming one!), but many men wished their mates wouldn't question their knowledge or argue with their decisions all the time. It's a touchy (and difficult) thing in these liberated days, but what it really comes down to is their need for us to defer to them sometimes.

I find that I can easily show respect on the positive side—for example, I can demonstrate that I respect Jeff by calling on his knowledge in a given subject. But sometimes it is a lot harder for me *not* to show *dis*respect. It takes a lot more effort to defer to his judgment when I want to seize control, since of course I think my way is right! In those scenarios, I can discover too late that my husband might have had a point—or I have argued an issue (and him) right into the ground. Can you relate?

Sadly, many men confessed that they felt as if their opinions and decisions were actively valued in every area of their lives *except* at home. In fact, several men explicitly told me that their comrades at work seemed to trust their judgment more than their own wives did. While a man's colleagues will rarely tell him what to do (asking, suggesting, or collaborating on the decision instead), more than one wife has fallen into the habit of ordering him around like one of the kids.

Early in my marriage, I unconsciously made that mistake far too many times. Jeff finally told me how stupid it made him feel, and hearing that was enough to shake me of the habit. On the surveys, many men said the one thing they wished they could tell their wives was to "show more trust in my decision-making abilities," which is code for (among other things) "I'm not stupid."

Need 2: Respect His Abilities

Another strong theme that emerged was that men want—even need—to figure things out for themselves. And if they can, they feel like they have conquered something and are affirmed as men. For some reason, spending hours figuring out how to put together the new DVD player is fun. Problem is, we want to help them. And guess how they interpret that? You got it: distrust. (It's a wonder *any* relationships work and that the human race didn't die out millennia ago!)

And, of course, our attention is not all benign. Sometimes we truly don't have confidence that our men can figure things out on their own. On the survey, one man wished he could tell his wife, "Have confidence in my general abilities of learning, application, fixing, rebuilding, repair, etc., without having to do it your way because you know it and think I do not."

> Problem is, we want to help them. And guess how they interpret that? You got it: distrust.

"Honey, Will You Please Just Ask...?"

It turns out that the old joke about men never wanting to stop and ask for directions is based on this truth—that men love figuring things out for themselves. If they can find their way through the hazards of the concrete jungle with only a tattered map and their wits, they feel like they've conquered something. They feel affirmed, excited, encouraged, alive.

Realizing that, now put yourself in your man's shoes and listen to this phrase: "Honey, can we *please* just stop and ask for directions?" While your overwhelming impulse is simply to get practical help, his is to conquer Everest, thank you very much. And here you are telling him you don't believe he can do it. And remember how important it is to a guy that his mate believes in him! When you tell him to ask for directions, you're telling him point-blank that you don't trust him to figure it out for himself.

Now, if you're like me, you're probably saying to yourself, "You're right, I don't! How on earth could he know how to find the highway entrance in this maze of streets?"

Well, there you have it, don't you? Are you going to decide to trust him or not? This particular "Will I trust him?" question is just a metaphor for all the little trust choices we make. I've talked to dozens of men about this, and here is their near-unanimous opinion: "Let him do it."

Several men said something like, "I'm not an idiot, okay? If I didn't think I could find what I was looking for, why would I be trying?" One said, "I may have no idea where I'm going. But it's fun; it's a challenge to try to find my own way. And I'm not stupid—I've got a clock on the dashboard. I know whether we're going to be late or not."

Little Things Add Up to One Big Clue

We don't realize that the act of forcing ourselves to trust our men in these little things means so much to them. But it does. It's not a big deal to us, so we don't get that it's a big deal to them. We don't get that our responses to these little choices to trust or not trust—or at least act like we do—are interpreted as signs of our overall trust and respect for them as men.

The next time your husband stubbornly drives in circles, ask yourself which is more important: being on time to the party or his feeling trusted? No contest.

> Next time your husband stubbornly drives in circles, ask yourself which is more important: being on time to the party or his feeling trusted?

Don't Tell Him How

The 1984 movie *The Natural* provides a powerful example of a woman's respect for a man.[1] Robert Redford plays an amazing baseball talent who, after mysteriously leaving his girlfriend and dropping out of sight for years, has finally gotten to the major leagues. After taking the world by storm, he suddenly hits a humiliating slump and starts doubting himself. In one powerful scene, his old flame watches from the stands as he strikes out again and again. When the dispirited Redford comes up for his final at bat, to scattered boos from the crowd, she suddenly stands up, alone, in the stands. Somehow he senses her presence, awakes from his slumber, and slams a home run, reigniting his passion and his game.

One man, explaining why he loves that scene, said, "She just stood up and supported him. She didn't come down from the stands and tell him what to do or how to fix what was wrong. She didn't tell him how to hold his bat. She just supported him and let *him* figure it out."

Another man agreed. "She stood up and publicly said, 'I know you can do it.' For any man, especially if he is in a season of self-doubt, that is exactly what he needs to be able to hit a home run in life."

> "She stood up and publicly said, 'I know you can do it.' For any man, that is exactly what he needs to be able to hit a home run."

Ladies, it is so easy for us to bristle at this idea and say, "Why can't I tell him how to hold his bat? We're equal partners! What if I know how better than he does?"

Well, of course, you *can* tell him. Most of us are perfectly competent to advise our men in all sorts of areas. But remember, he's the one up to bat, with his feeling of competency on the line.

True advice usually isn't a problem. But advice can quickly become instruction, and there we are again, trying to get in the batter's box and do it for him, implying that he can't do it himself.

Even thinking about this makes me cringe because it reminds me of the times I've inadvertently sent the message that I don't believe in my husband. Too often during Jeff's times of self-doubt with his business, I have tried to "support" him with advice—good, constructive advice, mind you. But I noticed that often demoralizes more than helps. To him, it meant that the person who knew him best didn't believe he could do it. What he most needed was for me to simply stand up and say, "I know you can do it." (See? I've been studying men for ten years and still mess up too often. Maybe in year eleven this will finally click…)

Some of you might be wondering, *But what if my man has so disappointed me that I feel that supporting him would just condone his mistakes?* If so, consider what another man pointed out: "That movie scene is a powerful illustration of what can happen when a woman chooses to honor and respect her man publicly, even when he may not deserve it. Instead of that choice somehow being demeaning or unfair to her, her act of showing respect lifted them both up."

Need 3: Respect What He Accomplishes

Now that you see how painful it is to a man to feel disrespected, and how important it is to him to figure things out on his own, perhaps you can see that very few things are as powerful to a man as feeling that he has tried something, accomplished it, done it well—and someone noticed.

I didn't see how profound this need was until a few years after the original edition came out, when my friend Lisa Rice and I were researching *For Parents Only*. We found that girls and women tended to have deep, hidden questions like, *Am I special? Am I lovable?* and thus needed to feel special and worthy of being loved for who they were on the inside. But the men and boys really didn't have those questions. Instead, they worried, *Do I measure up? Am I any good at what I do?* In other words: they deeply need to feel noticed, able, and appreciated for what they do on the outside.

> We women need to feel special and worthy
> of being loved for who we are on the inside.
> Men need to feel able and appreciated for
> what they do on the outside.

As strange as it sounds to us, saying "You did a great job at that meeting" or "You are such a great dad" is far more emotionally powerful to a man than hearing "I love you." In the survey for my upcoming book, *Seven Secrets of Highly Happy Marriages,* more than seven out of ten men said that if their wives simply noticed something and said thank you, it had a big impact on their happiness level.

When (or if) your wife does the [action] below, choose the impact [it] has on you, in terms of how happy or "filled up" it makes you:

Noticing when I do something and sincerely thanking me for it. (For example, "Thank you for mowing the lawn even though it was so hot outside" or "Thanks for playing with the kids, even when you were so tired from work.") (Choose one answer.)

It deeply pleases me—it's a small thing that has a relatively big impact.	72%
It feels nice, but not much impact.	26%
It doesn't do much for me.	2%

0%   50%   100%

I cannot tell you the number of times a man has shared how secretly painful it is when his wife tries to thank him but instead sends the (accidental!) signal "But it wasn't good enough." As one man told me, "She'll come into the kitchen after I've finished wiping down all the countertops. I'm proud it looks so good, and she'll say, 'Thanks, honey. Oh, but you missed the crumbs under the toaster.' Under the toaster! I know she doesn't mean 'You've failed,' but privately it just kills me."

Many women have been confused about why their men would say, "Nothing I do is good enough for you." *Huh?* Well, guess what: that is a giant red flag. Without realizing it, we've been sending them the ultimate in painful messages: "You tried... and failed."

Thankfully, even simple appreciation (if it is undiluted by criticism) is powerful. One of my favorite speaking formats is when pastors interview me on these subjects at sermon time. One Sunday I was with Andy Stanley, pastor of North Point Community Church near Atlanta, when he relayed to the congregation something I'll never forget—a conversation where he told his wife, "If you never told me that you loved me again, but throughout our marriage you simply told me how proud you are...I'm not sure I would miss 'I love you' because of what it means in my heart to hear that you're proud of me. It is that big of a deal."

Need 4: Respect in Communication

Women wield incredible power in the way we communicate with our men (including our sons)—power to build up or to tear down, to encourage or to exasperate. Some things just push a man's buttons or are extremely painful in ways we don't realize. This goes beyond *what* we say, such as questioning a man's judgment or his abilities, and into *how* we say it (and *where* we say it, which is the subject of the next section).

> Some things just push a man's buttons or are painful. This goes beyond what we say—and into how we say it.

In interviews, a large number of men said something like, "When my wife says something disrespectful, I often think, *I can't believe she doesn't know how that makes me feel!*" I had to reassure these men over and over that their wives probably didn't mean to disrespect them and were likely just clueless.

Let me give you several common examples of how a man might hear something negative where the woman never intended it.

Hearing Disrespect

At one point I was asking Jeff and one of his married colleagues about the dynamic of men wanting to do things for themselves. This man said, "Sometimes, if something breaks in the house, I want to try to take a crack at it before I call an expert. If my wife says, 'Well, you're really not a fix-it–type person,' I feel so insulted. She's not rude about it or anything, but it's like she doesn't respect me enough to believe that I can figure it out if I put my mind to it, even if it takes me a while."

This man's wife is one of my closest friends, and I know that she fully respects her husband. So it was an eyeopener to hear that what was (to her) an offhand remark was something he took extremely seriously—and, if I may delicately say so, extremely wrong.

Hearing Disappointment

In the survey, as in life, a sizable minority of men read something negative into a simple female reminder. I asked men what would go through their minds if their wives or significant others reminded them that the kitchen wall was damaged and it still had to be fixed. More than one-third of these men took that reminder as nagging or as an accusation of laziness or mistrust.

Early in the research, I met with my friend and book agent, Calvin Edwards, at Starbucks to start designing the original survey questions. When we saw a local pastor Calvin knew, I ran the "kitchen wall" question by him and asked what would go through his mind. Consider his illuminating response:

> *Pastor:* I'm irritated because I have to be reminded. I hate being reminded.
> *Calvin:* Why is that a problem? Look at your day planner

there—you set up systems to remind yourself of things all the time.

Pastor: Inherent in her reminder is a statement of disappointment. For me as a man, that is saying that I failed. I hate to fail. It's not the statement that bothers me; it's the implications of the statement.

Now, it's interesting that those who jumped to negative conclusions were still in the minority. A larger group—fully half of the men polled—simply didn't place as high a priority on the task as their wives did and said it would get done eventually.

Hearing Attacks

I got an excellent example of how our words can be misinterpreted as an attack when Chuck Cowan and I were discussing a survey question I had drafted: "Do you know how to put together a romantic event that your partner would enjoy?"

Chuck: That question won't work because you're starting off in attack mode.

Me: Huh?

Chuck: You're starting off suggesting the man is inept.

Me (thinking to myself): *Suggesting the man is inept? What is he talking about?*

Chuck: Soften it a bit—put it into a context that isn't so
blatant.

Simply by adding a context sentence to the beginning—
"Suppose you had to plan an anniversary event for your partner.
Do you know how...?"—the question was softer and deemed
just fine to not question a man's adequacy.

No matter what we think we are saying, in the end what matters is what the guy is hearing. Now, obviously, some people can
be overly sensitive, and we can't walk on eggshells all the time. Nor
do we want to pass up all opportunities to help men understand
our communication wiring. But considering that most men appear to be highly sensitive to disrespect—including seeing it where
none is intended—I would argue that it is not the average man
who needs to be less sensitive to a woman's words, but the average
woman who needs to be more sensitive to her man's feelings.

> No matter what we think we are saying, in
> the end what matters is what the guy is
> hearing.

After all, don't we want our men to adjust to *our* sensitivities?
Do you want your husband to publicly tease you about gaining
ten pounds? It's all about loving each other the way the other
person needs to be loved.

Need 5: Respect in Public

There is an epidemic of public disrespect for men today, and the biggest culprit is not television, movies, or other media but the women who are supposed to love their men most.

"The Most Fragile Thing on the Planet"

Dozens of men told me how painful it is when their wives or girlfriends criticize them in public, put them down, or even question their judgment in front of others. One very representative man on the survey said that the one thing he wished he could tell his wife was that "at a minimum, she should be supportive of me in public."

> Dozens of men told me how painful it is when their wives or girlfriends criticize them in public.

Consider this statement, which I have heard (in essence) from many men: "My wife says things about me in public that she considers teasing. I consider them torture."

One married man put it starkly: "The male ego is the most fragile thing on the planet. Women have this thought that *He's got such a huge ego that I need to take him down a peg.* No way. The male ego is incredibly fragile."

We women often think of this as male pride—but that isn't

it. What is at stake isn't his pride as much as his secret feelings of inadequacy as a man. There's a big difference between feeling prideful and feeling adequate. What happens in public isn't that his "inflated" pride is brought down to ground level but that something made him feel inadequate and humiliated as a man. Disrespect in public is so painful that men will avoid it at any cost. In fact, many unmarried men described it as a major (if unseen) factor leading to a breakup instead of marriage. As one twenty-something man told me, "I don't want to live with that for the rest of my life."

Teasing Can Be Torture

Even good-natured teasing can sometimes be humiliating, not to mention more pointed jabs. Many of us have wondered why men who normally have a great sense of humor get upset by a little public joking at their expense. I was writing the original version of this chapter at my computer one day over the holidays, and my parents were around. I asked my dad a question, and my husband came into the office as we were talking. The resulting discussion was so fascinating—and foundational—that I started typing it into my file. Here is a portion:

> *Me:* What sort of teasing might a man take wrong?
> *Dad:* Anything that seems to show that the man is not
> somehow in control or not getting respect from his

wife. A man would never take that from another man, unless he wanted a fight.

Me: But what if she's truly teasing? Like they're out with friends, and the wife says, "Oh, the dishwasher broke," and she teases her husband about wanting to fix it when he's not a handyman?

Dad: Oh, that's terrible. You never want to do that. The guy is the protector, provider, and is supposed to take care of everything. This sort of teasing lets everyone know that he doesn't know how to take care of everything. It also lets everyone know how the wife feels about him—she's making light of something that is really important to him! But if a guy feels that he ought to be able to do something as the provider and he can't, he never makes light of it in his heart.

Jeff: It all depends on whether that particular guy already feels inadequate in that area. That same thing may not hit another man wrong.

Me: Does it make a difference if the wife is teasing him in front of men or women?

Dad: Oh, it's much worse in front of men. After an incident early on in our marriage, I asked your mom, "Please don't *ever* embarrass me in front of another man."

Me: Why?

Dad: Guys are always in competition with one another.

Your wife is the person who knows you better than anyone, and if she doesn't respect you, how can you expect another man to?

Jeff: It's also humiliating to know that the other guy feels sorry for me because my wife doesn't respect me.

Dad: Even worse, if the other man doesn't know you well, it is a sign of weakness. The other man is thinking, *If this guy's own wife doesn't respect him, he's nothing. We'll run him over the next time we do a deal together.* If you belittle your husband in front of another man, you can even ruin his career. I'm not kidding. Because any man he works with will now see him as weak.

Me: Back to the teasing question…

Dad: You have to understand—men don't let down their guards easily, particularly with other men, unless they are very close. Most men probably crave a situation where they can, but they aren't naturally made that way—it's all a competition instead. The only time a guy's guard is completely down is with the woman he loves. So she can pierce his heart like no one else.

"The only time a guy's guard is completely down is with the woman he loves. So she can pierce his heart like no one else."

Showing Public Respect Goes a Long Way

Learning how important public respect is to men, I have become much more sensitive to how often we talk negatively about them behind their backs. Not just because it matters to them, but because it affects how we feel about them: the more we express dissatisfaction, the more deeply it lodges in our hearts. I have a dear friend who loves her husband but also regularly complains about him. I'm convinced that's one of the main reasons she can't shake a nagging dissatisfaction with their relationship—a dissatisfaction that then affects him.

But on the positive side, just as your man is hurt by public disrespect, so will he think you are the most wonderful woman in the world if you publicly build him up. This is not artificial; you simply take those little opportunities to honestly praise him or to ask his opinion in front of others. Do you think he's a great father? Tell your dinner guests a story about something he did with the kids yesterday that proves it. Are you impressed with his managerial acumen? Brag on the way he solved a crisis at work. Did he take the kids out and let you sleep in Saturday morning? Tell your book club and make the other girls jealous.

Trust me—from the men I've talked to, that is the equivalent of his coming home to you with a dozen roses and a surprise date night without the kids. He will feel *adored*.

Need 6: Respect in Our Assumptions

Unfortunately, in one area, men have every right to read something negative into what we say. Listen to what you say to him or assume about him over the next few days. You may be astounded at how often you assume something bad. See if any of these negative assumptions ring a bell.

We Assume He Needs to be Reminded

To us, repeatedly asking "Have you done it yet?" doesn't seem like a big deal. But inherent in the question is our assumption that guys need the reminder—that they are either incapable of remembering on their own or that they remember but need our prodding to do the job. It's no wonder many men hate being nagged. What they are accurately hearing is "I don't trust you."

Instead, what if we were to assume the best of them rather than the worst? For example: *I asked him to do it. He hasn't done it. I trust my husband. Therefore, there's a* reason *he hasn't done it.*

Just realize, although his reason for not doing the task may be different from yours, that makes it no less legitimate. Remember, half the men on the survey indicated that sometimes they just have different priorities than their wives do. Or they could just be unable to handle one more thing. Remember the "kitchen wall" question I posed to the pastor at Starbucks? Here's how he put it:

I've revealed something about my preferences and priorities by *not* fixing it for a week. If I come home with the world on my shoulders—if a couple at church is divorcing or I'm worried that a key employee might leave—and my wife is in her house mode and says the living room fern is dying, that is hard for me to engage in. The brutal truth is that it's not as important to me. My first response is, "Get a fern doctor." But Scripture says that as a husband, I have to lay down my life for my wife, so sometimes I have to talk about the fern. But we have a little code now, where I'll tell her it's "fern doctor stuff" to let her know that sometimes my brain just doesn't go there.

We Assume He's Choosing Not to Help

A marriage counselor shared this example: "If my husband doesn't help with the kids or the cleaning, I shouldn't assume that he sees it and is choosing not to help. I should start with the assumption that he doesn't see it."

It turns out that avoiding this assumption is important for more than just our man's well-being. In my recent research, I found that one of the main reasons happy couples are so happy is because they always try to assume that their spouses have good intentions toward them.

We Assume It's Because of Him

Finally (and this may be a shocking thought), some things are not his fault—*they're ours.* We can assign unloving motives to our men for actions that can actually be traced back to something we have inadvertently said or done. For example, a wife who is constantly critical of her husband may spur him to withdraw emotionally to protect himself, thereby becoming unloving where he wasn't before.

"Men are not stupid," says Dr. Eggerichs. "They are not Neanderthals. Sometimes these behaviors that appear to be unloving are not unloving at all. They are reacting that way because they interpret something as disrespect. Even if sometimes they shouldn't."

SO WHAT SHOULD WE DO?

We as women hold incredible power. And responsibility. And opportunity. We have the ability to either build up or tear down our men. We can either strengthen or hobble them in ways that go far beyond our relationship, because respect at home affects every area of a man's life. There is something in how a man approaches the world that makes his inner, home-fired feelings of personal adequacy absolutely foundational to everything else.

So what should we do? As one man powerfully put it, "Always assume the best, and you will find it easier to show respect." Simple as it sounds, from now on we can choose to show that we appreciate, trust, and respect the men in our lives, and choose *not* to demonstrate disrespect, starting with never humiliating them in public.

If there are areas in which you find it difficult to trust your man, realize that you can be respectful even when you are wrestling with a real area of concern. Don't ignore problems, but find things you can appreciate and applaud regardless. The apostle Paul advised the Christians in Philippi to choose to "rejoice" by focusing on whatever is good and worthy of praise.

In fact, given how positively motivated a man is by his woman believing in him, and how demotivated he is by the sense that she doesn't, verbally praising the positives is *especially* vital for a man who needs to overcome past failure.

And when we realize that *we* have messed up—maybe for years—we can acknowledge our fault and ask for forgiveness. In my years of speaking on the importance of respect to a man, I have been so touched to see how forgiving most men are when wives or girlfriends suddenly get it. I have had dozens of men come up to me in private, with tears of gratitude, to tell me something like, "She came home last night and said, 'I'm so sorry. I had no idea how much I was hurting you.' I can't tell you how much that meant to me."

As we move forward, we'll inevitably blow it sometimes. We'll see the anger or withdrawal that signals our men are suffering the pain of our disrespect. But when that happens, men recommended we avoid saying, "I'm sorry I made you *feel* XYZ" (since, as one man put it, "That implies 'I wasn't disrespectful, and you shouldn't feel that way'"). Instead, they recommended simply saying something like, "I'm really sorry I said that—it was disrespectful. I know I can trust you."

It's Not Just for Them, but for Us

Consider this man's plea: "She has to make me feel respected so that I can command respect out in the world. If she defeats me emotionally, I can't win the race and bring home the prize for her."

Another man told me, "You know that saying 'Behind every good man is a great woman'? Well, that is *so true*. If a man's wife is supportive and believes in him, he can conquer the world—or at least his little corner of it. He will do better at work, at home, everywhere. By contrast, very few men can do well at work *or* at home if their wives make them feel inadequate."

> "If a man's wife believes in him, he can conquer the world—or at least his little corner of it."

As you now have glimpsed, inside their confident exterior many men are vulnerable and even insecure. That is the subject of the next chapter.

---

* To avoid confusion, be aware that I am using the words *girlfriend, significant other,* and *partner* interchangeably, with no particular meaning as to age, seriousness of the relationship, or living arrangements. For consistency, I used the words *wife / significant other* throughout the surveys.

Three

THE PERFORMANCE
OF A LIFETIME

Why Your Mr. Smooth Looks
So Impressive but Feels Like
an Impostor

*Despite their "in control" exterior, men
often feel like impostors and are insecure
that their inadequacies will be discovered.*

$\mathbb{A}$t the risk of admitting that I am a closet Trekkie, let me take
you to an old episode of *Star Trek: The Next Generation*.[2] The
confident captain, Jean-Luc Picard, and his friend Dr. Beverly
Crusher are (of course) stuck on a dangerous and unfamiliar
planet. And their predicament has an interesting twist: because of
some alien meddling, the two can hear each other's thoughts.

As the captain leads them toward help, he scans the unfamiliar horizon, motions in a particular direction, and says, with his usual commanding certainty, "This way."

Since she can hear what he is actually thinking, the doctor stares at him and says, "You don't really know, do you? You're acting like you know exactly which way to go, but you're only guessing!" Then, with growing amazement, she asks, "Do you do this all the time?"

He gives her a look, then answers, "There are times when it is necessary for a captain to give the appearance of confidence." Dr. Crusher had just discovered what most of us never grasp—that the men in our lives are hiding a deep sense of self-doubt.

> Dr. Crusher had just discovered what most of us never grasp—that the men in our lives are hiding a deep self-doubt.

This inner uncertainty leaves even the most confident-seeming man dreading the moment when he will be exposed for who he really is—or at least believes himself to be.

An impostor.

"THEY ARE GOING TO FIND ME OUT!"

Most men have an inner vulnerability that we don't even know is there, stemming from a set of competing core needs and fears.

Something deep inside them wants to tackle a great challenge and try difficult things…but at the same time, they find the idea of failing excruciating. One of their greatest emotional needs is to feel competent and successful at what they do, especially in front of others…but at the same time, they have a deep conviction that what they do is always being watched and judged. Hence the reason for this deep, unseen insecurity: they so deeply want to succeed but feel that they are one mess-up from being found out.

In all my surveys, no matter how I asked the question, no matter how successful a man was, and no matter how secure they looked on the outside, around three-fourths admitted to this insecurity about whether they could hack it and what others think of them. Whether it was about being a good husband, father, mechanic, businessman, or student, they deeply wanted to do well, and tried to look confident but felt insecure.

Look at the stark results from the national survey I conducted for my workplace book *The Male Factor* when I asked if the men ever instinctively felt certain ways:

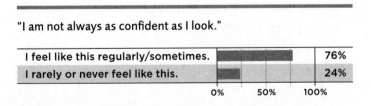

"I am not always as confident as I look."

I feel like this regularly/sometimes.	76%
I rarely or never feel like this.	24%

0%   50%   100%

Just as the heart cry of a woman tends to be, *Am I loveable?* the secret heart cry of a man is, *Do I measure up?* And he is looking to those around him—especially the woman who knows him best—for clues to the answer to that question.

In one follow-up survey I did with four hundred church-goers, 72 percent of the men said, "I try to perform well and look as competent as possible, when inside I sometimes feel insecure and am concerned about others' opinion of me and my abilities."

To compensate for his insecurity—and his feeling of being watched—a man may feel the need to work long hours to prove to his wife that he can provide for his family. Or he may get emotionally worn down by the constant need to look on the ball at work.

One thing is certain: the idea of someone thinking he can't cut it is humiliating—a feeling every man wants to avoid at all costs. So he puts up a good front so others will think he's highly competent. And there we are, back at the beginning. In the spotlight stands a man—maybe your husband—feeling sure that if anyone (even his wife) really knew him for what he was, they'd know the truth. The truth that—at least some of the time—he is not what he appears to be.

The idea of someone thinking he can't cut it is humiliating—a feeling every man wants to avoid at all costs.

WHAT'S DRIVING HIM?

You and I watch the men in our lives go off to work every day, joke with friends, and take physical risks without flinching. And if you're like me, it never once crosses your mind that he lacks confidence, that deep inside he feels like a poser. *I have full confidence in him and his abilities,* you think. *Why wouldn't* he*?* But the facts show that he doesn't. Here's what the surveys show he's really feeling.

"I'm Always Being Judged"

Men told me they are hard enough on themselves without any external pressure. Add in the conviction that the eyes of the world are critically trained on them, and you suddenly see how uncomfortable and insecure they might feel. One man put it this way: "We think about what others think about us *all the time*." One male friend shared an amusing anecdote that perfectly captured this myopic male certainty:

> When I was in college, I drove one of the school transit
> buses part-time to earn money. Sometimes, when I had
> no one on board, I drove—um—rather quickly. One day
> I came hurtling around a corner, and there was an elderly
> man standing at the bus stop, shaking his head no at me.

It irritated me that he was disapproving of my driving! Years later I lived in New York City, and one day I shook my head no to tell an approaching bus driver not to stop because I didn't need his particular route. Suddenly it hit me: All those years ago that elderly man had just been saying no, he didn't need my route. Instead, I built up this whole assumption that he had examined my performance and found me wanting. That is a silly example, but it's what every guy does.

This man went on to clarify, "It's your abilities *and* you that are being judged. Men aren't always as sure of themselves as they look. That's why, when your wife makes a joke at your expense in front of other people, it's a knife."

"I Have No Earthly Idea How to Do This"

Another male friend illustrated the impostor complex with this story:

A young friend of mine had just gotten a job as a college professor. He had never done these particular lesson plans, so he was running to stay one step ahead of his students. Often he would literally be one day ahead of them in the textbook. One evening, one of his students ran into him on campus and said she was looking forward to his class in the morning. She said, "I wish I knew as much as you do about this stuff." He smiled and nodded, but inside he was thinking, *Tomorrow, you will!*

My friend said, "That is a perfect description of how many men feel as they go through life, especially whenever they do something unfamiliar—which most of us have to do all the time. A client may be asking me to do something new, and I may be smiling and nodding, but in the back of my mind, I'm thinking, *I have no earthly idea how to do this, and I hope I can learn it before they find out.*"

What was startling about this conversation is that I have worked with this man for years, and he is an extremely competent businessman. I had originally thought that maybe this dynamic only affected younger, less-experienced men. But hearing the same thing from those who are highly accomplished helped me realize just how deep-seated this vulnerability is.

"But I Want to Do This!"

The doubt our men experience regarding their ability to pull things off has an interesting partner—their deep desire to take on something new and exciting. These two feelings may seem contradictory, but they are all part of the male package. Men t (or at least the mean streets of the city), y risk taking a humiliating tumble on the this way:

When ___ es something that he's never done before and he's being paid for it, he thinks, *I can do this, but what if they find out this is my first time?* There's a joke among some guys that you're going to be talking in front of a group sometime, and your fourth-grade teacher's going to run in and say, "He doesn't know what he's talking about! He was a D student!" It's this irrational, debilitating fear that you'll publicly be found out. And sooner or later, every man has to face it. Because if you want to move up, that will inevitably mean doing something new.

As you might guess, those times—whether at work or at home—are when men feel the shakiest and need the most encouragement from us.

THE IMPOSTOR AT WORK

A man's uncertainty about his adequacy on the job can take a huge toll. One man said, "We have incredible anxiety over where we stand at work. I start to think that the fact that my boss isn't communicating with me means that he's found me out. This creates intense anxiety and uncertainty."

"I Want to See You First Thing Monday Morning..."

Frank Maguire helped start Federal Express and earlier held an inside position in the Kennedy White House. His book *You're the Greatest* takes us inside the unique torture of a man's workplace anxiety.

Every Friday as he left the FedEx office, Maguire called his good-byes to FedEx founder, Fred Smith, and Fred would call back, "Thanks for going the extra mile this week." Maguire always left with a bounce in his step.

Then came the Friday when his cheery good-bye was met with, "Frank, I want to see you first thing, Monday morning."

"I had a lousy weekend," Maguire said. "Not only me, but my wife, my kids, even Thor, the wonder dog. We all had a miserable weekend."

On Monday, when he nervously asked Fred, "What did you want to talk to me about?" he was met with a puzzled look. "Oh, I forgot. It wasn't important."

You can guess why Frank Maguire had a miserable weekend—he was expecting to be fired. But why would he think that? He was a successful, valued executive at a fast-growing business. He had even been trusted by the president of the United States. So why did he assume a neutral comment was a portent of woe?

Because inside he felt like an impostor. And he was sure he had just been found out.

> Inside he felt like an impostor. And he was sure he had just been found out.

Maguire wrote, "I've been around many powerful leaders. On the surface, they looked totally secure. You would never guess there was even one ounce of fear. But my experience has also convinced me that no matter what your title or position in life is, we all, no exceptions, carry our treasures in fragile containers."[3]

"We're All on the Replacement List"

One of the most revealing interviews I conducted was with Ken Ruettgers, a former all-pro offensive tackle with the Super Bowl champion Green Bay Packers. He now helps retiring athletes make the difficult transition into well-balanced, regular lives.

When I told him the subject of this chapter, he jumped on it. "I've never seen so many insecurities as in the locker room," he said. Surprised, I asked him why. Here's his explanation:

Because the guys are naked on the field. They have two or three hours to prove themselves, and there's no fooling the camera. Once you look through the mask, you've got the most insecure guys ever. They try to put up a great front, but once they know each other really well, they'll ask, "How'd I do on that play?" They are just looking for affirmation.

And it's not just the camera—it's the knowledge that some guys are going to get cut. [Another all-pro football player] put it this way: "We're all on the replacement list. You just want to stay off the top of it."

You know, sports is like corporate America—there's a "What have you done for me lately?" attitude. It's incredibly draining, and there is a huge, unspoken fear of failure.

Ken went on to make an important point. "Keep in mind that guys can use that fear of failure for good. It gets you out of bed in the morning. It gets you to the gym when you wouldn't go otherwise."

Ken's words helped me realize why so many men—talented, effective men—work such long hours. Sometimes the long hours are a necessity for the job. But not always. Sometimes they are (in the guy's mind) an insurance against fear—fear of falling behind, fear of being cut from the team.

THE IMPOSTOR AT HOME

One of the things that surprised me the most in all my research was that a man's performance anxiety doesn't, as one man put it, "just end when we walk through the front door." Many feel just as inadequate at home. The majority of men do want to be good husbands. But in the same way they worry that they may not know everything about being a good employee, they secretly worry that they don't know how to succeed at being a good husband, father, provider, or handyman.

"At least at work," one man told me, "I have an idea of how to succeed—work hard, get ahead, complete assignments, and get in good with the boss. At home, what is the measure of success? How do I know whether I am a success or a failure?"

Not surprisingly, men said they judge themselves—and feel that others judge them—based on the happiness and respect of their wives.

If a man feels like he's trying to bluff his way through this being-a-husband thing, you can imagine his relief when he can tell that his wife feels loved and happy, or when she publicly honors him and his "husband abilities." And conversely, you can imagine the trepidation he feels when he receives the cold shoulder confirmation that he got it wrong again, that he is indeed an impostor, that he doesn't know what he's doing in his personal life. One man wrote me a note about this:

I don't know one man who thinks he has all the answers when it comes to being a good father or husband. If we've had good fathers, then we try and remember what our fathers would do in the situation. If we didn't have good fathers, we feel like we're making it up as we go. If my wife often challenges my decisions or appears displeased with me as a husband—it's the impostor all over again. It may even cause a man to withdraw from taking an active role in the lives of his wife and kids if he doesn't think he can do it well or be affirmed in it. That's not a rational or Christlike approach by the man, for sure, but that is how some guys feel.

> "I don't know one man who thinks he has all the answers when it comes to being a good father or husband."

WHAT SHOULD WE DO?

So what on earth can we do about this? You and I aren't responsible for changing how a man is wired. But we can certainly affect how he feels about his ability to make his way in the world. In particular, as you have probably guessed by now, men's private doubt about whether they measure up is the reason why our respect (chapter 2) matters so much to them. Once we understand what our husbands secretly feel and think, our words and actions can make a huge difference.

"Affirmation Is Everything"

Have you ever noticed how the adulterous woman in the book of Proverbs seduces the unwitting young man? It's not with sex (okay, not *just* with sex); it's with flattery. "She threw her arms around him...and with a brazen look she said, 'I've offered my sacrifices and just finished my vows. It's you I was looking for!'.... With her flattery she enticed him. He followed her at once."

Flattery is simply a seductive counterfeit for affirmation. As one marriage counselor told me, "Affirmation is everything. When a man is affirmed, he can conquer the world. When he's not, he is sapped of his confidence and even his feeling of manhood. And believe me, he will, consciously or unconsciously, seek out places where he receives affirmation."

Fortunately for us, home is by far the most important place for a man to be affirmed. If a man knows that the person who knows him best believes in him, he is empowered to do better in every area of his life. A man tends to think of life as a competition and a battle, and he can go duke it out if he can come home to someone who supports him unconditionally, who will wipe his brow and tell him he can do it. As one of our close friends told me, "It's all about whether my wife thinks I can do it. A husband can slay dragons, climb mountains, and win great victories if *he* believes his *wife* believes that he can."

Don't Tear Him Down!

If, instead of affirming, a wife reinforces her husband's feelings of inadequacy, it can become a self-fulfilling prophecy. For example, if she focuses her attention on what he is doing wrong in the relationship, she can unwittingly undermine what she most wants—for him to do it right.

> Of the men I surveyed, only one man in four felt actively appreciated by his family.

But I discovered a dismaying fact. Of the men on my main survey, only one man in four felt actively appreciated by his family. And 44 percent of men actually felt unappreciated at home. More pointedly, men in their prime years of responsibility for home, children, and work—men between the ages of thirty-six and fifty-five—felt even less appreciated.

I'll bet that many of the wives or girlfriends of these men would be surprised to learn that they didn't feel appreciated. My guess is that most of us *do* appreciate our men but don't show it enough.

If a man isn't convinced that his woman thinks he's the

greatest, he will tend to seek affirmation elsewhere. He may spend more hours at work, where he feels alive and on top of his game, or he may spend too much time talking to the admiring female associate. He may immerse himself in watching or playing sports, feeling the thrill of the competitive rush. Or he may retreat to his workshop or his home office, feeling as if he can control things there even if he feels inadequate and clumsy elsewhere.

"Why else do you think so many men take sports so seriously?" one man asked me. "It's something they feel good at, something they've practiced. They are admired and encouraged by other men on the field. People say 'Good hit!' or 'Good shot!' or show by tightening their defense that they know you're about to smoke them. There's nothing like that feeling. But I feel that same way at home when my wife applauds me for bringing in a big business deal or brags to her friends about what a good father I am. It's that same feeling."

During my clinical research for *The Lights of Tenth Street*, several experts told me that the chronic feeling of not measuring up is a major reason men fall into pornography addiction. For whatever reason, they feel like less than a man, so they seek—and find—affirmation in pornography. As one man pointed out, "All those women in the men's magazines and porn sites convey one message: 'I want *you*, and you are the most desirable man in the world.' My wife may be nagging me at home, the kids may be disobedient, and I may be worried about messing up at work, but looking at the woman in that picture makes me feel like a *man*."

"All those women in the men's magazines convey one message: 'I want you, and you are the most desirable man in the world.'"

If affirmation does indeed carry so much power, why should a man have to look for it in other places when he has a wife who loves and respects him? There's nothing wrong with work, sports, or hobbies—it's wonderful for him to feel alive and encouraged in those pursuits. But they shouldn't have to be a retreat from an *un*affirming home life.

Create a Safety Zone

Obviously, if many of our men spend their workdays feeling like they are always being watched and judged, it is no wonder that they want to come home to a totally accepting environment, where they can safely let their guard down. Men need a place where they can make their mistakes in peace and not constantly worry that they are one misstep away from being exposed.

If we don't realize this, then it is so easy in the day-to-day hustle and bustle to notice only our men's mistakes ("I can't believe you forgot the dry cleaning *again*"). If that becomes a pattern, we risk creating a situation that is the opposite of what we want. Most of us want our men to be able to relax and truly open up to us. But in many ways, it is up to us to create the intimate, safe environment that makes that possible.

We may think that the adage "His home must be his haven" is antiquated and unnecessary these days, but that is far from the truth. In fact, as the workplace has gotten harsher and less loyal, more demanding and less tolerant of mistakes, I'd say it's even more important that a man's home be a haven. Most of the men I talked with crave a retreat from the daily pressure of always having to perform.

> Most of the men I talked with crave a retreat from the daily pressure of always having to perform.

Supportive Sex

Okay, girls, don't keel over from surprise when I tell you that this particular type of affirmation came up again and again. We'll talk more about how men view sex in a separate chapter, but I owe it to the many husbands who commented on its importance to mention it here.

"Sex plays a *hu-u-u-u-uge* role in a man's self-confidence!" reported one husband via e-mail. "A man can be having a horrible time at work, rejection in his industry, and every other area can be going rotten—but if his wife wants him physically and affirms him in bed, he can handle the rest of the world, no problem. Conversely, if he gets the same impostor message at home ('You don't measure up. Don't touch me'), it will devastate him far worse than any career blow."

Another man said, "The role of sex cannot be overstated. A great sex life will overshadow and overcome a multitude of impostor messages from the world."

THE GIFT OF CONFIDENCE

I heard from many men, "Men put a lot of pressure on themselves." On the survey, one husband pleaded, "I want my wife to know and understand my weaknesses, failings, shortcomings, and still want me. I need her to be my number-one source of encouragement to become the man God created me to be." We might think we wouldn't have the ability to change our men's feelings of workplace inadequacy, but we would be wrong. By staunchly supporting our men, showing that we believe in them, and providing an emotionally safe environment to come home to, we can help give them confidence to dive back into the workplace fray.

In his autobiography, Jack Welch, the famous chairman and CEO of General Electric, provides an insight for businessmen that is important for every wife—and mother—to hear. Speaking about his mother, he wrote,

> Perhaps the greatest single gift she gave me was self-confidence. It's what I've looked for and tried to build in every executive who has ever worked with me. Confidence gives you courage and extends your reach. It lets you take greater risks and achieve far more than you ever thought possible. Building self-confidence in others is a huge part of leadership. It comes from providing opportunities and challenges for people to do things they never imagined they could do— rewarding them after each success in every way possible.[4]

It's about sending the men we love into the world every day, alive with the belief that they can slay dragons.

A wife can give her husband that confidence. It's not about being the supportive "little woman." It's about realizing that, despite their veneer of confidence, our men really do "carry their treasures in fragile containers," and they crave our affirmation for whether they "done good." It's about sending the men we love into the world every day, alive with the belief that they can slay dragons.

Four

THE THINKER

When Checking Out Is Actually Checking In

Men address issues by first
pulling away to process and think—
so they can better talk about them later.

A few years after the original edition of this book was released, I was at my desk working when the phone rang. It was a dear friend in another city, seven months pregnant with her second child, in tears after an argument with her husband. Each of them had hurt the other's feelings, and when the conflict escalated, her husband had quietly left the house and driven away.

"I can't handle this anymore—he's done this several times," she sobbed. "How can he do this to me? He must not love me very much."

One thing about writing these books about the inner lives of men is that I sometimes find myself very able to see things from the guy's point of view—and it's not always comfortable. Feeling like a traitor, I asked my friend, "Um, when you and he had your first big conflict, did he end up leaving the room?"

I could hear the sniffles on the other end of the line. "Yes. Can you believe that? I told him exactly how he made me feel, and instead of talking about it, he wanted to walk away! I know he was upset with me too, but he wouldn't even explain why!"

"Uh…and did you follow him and continue to ask him questions about what he was thinking?"

"Yes! But he wouldn't answer me. He said he didn't want to talk yet. He just seemed to shut down—like he didn't even care that he hurt my feelings."

I told her that I was pretty sure why he had left the house and that it had nothing to do with him not caring. She listened in surprise as I shared my guess that he had probably left *because* he cared about her but couldn't figure out how to respond in the moment. Her emotions had probably flustered him. Then he probably got angry that he was flustered and couldn't think clearly. And then, I suggested, he most likely felt he couldn't risk saying or doing *anything* for fear of hurting her even more. All he could do was escape.

The next day she told me that when her husband had returned, he had explained it in almost that exact way—and she realized he had tried to get the point across plenty of times before, but she had never really understood what he was saying.

Much to my friend's surprise, I laughed. "Join the club!"

WHAT I DIDN'T SEE BEFORE

My husband is a thoughtful guy, but in the first half of our marriage, I often found myself completely baffled or hurt during a conflict by how Jeff communicated with me. Or didn't.

A typical scenario might have gone something like this: We'd stumble into a disagreement or misunderstanding. We'd each try to make—and win—our point. Temperatures would rise. Soon I'd feel hurt (he would too). But more than anything, I'd feel a huge need to talk things out.

Right then, though, Jeff would want to step away.

But why? We'd both been told in premarital counseling how dangerous it was to *not* communicate when there was conflict!

My reaction would be to pursue him. Upset, I'd follow him down the hallway, asking him something like, "Well, what do you think about what I just said? Don't leave before we've worked this out! At least tell me what you're feeling!"

But instead of talking, he would head downstairs, face tight, aiming for the solace of his home office. "I don't know what I'm thinking, and I just can't talk about it," he'd say and disappear, leaving me shattered that my usually loving husband suddenly didn't care enough to engage on such an important issue.

Any of that sound familiar?

As our research continued, Jeff and I realized that a big truth was hiding underneath the stormy surface of these conflicts. A truth that applies not just to conflict but to all areas of verbal communication—and can dramatically reduce how often conflict happens in the first place.

You see, caring husbands or boyfriends want to communicate with the women they love. But how they need to go about it is likely to be very different from the way you or I automatically prefer. Understanding that difference offers great promise for our relationships, and that difference is what this chapter—new for this edition—is all about.

> Men want to communicate with the women they love, but how they need to go about it is likely to be very different.

READING HIS SIGNALS IN A NEW LIGHT

We've all heard comments similar to these from a husband, boyfriend, or son:

- (frustrated) "I don't know what I'm thinking right now!"
- (wearily) "I just need a few minutes to decompress before you hit me with your day."
- (angrily) "I figured it out already, okay!"
- (pleading) "Can we *please* talk about this later?"
- (in front of the television) "Sorry, honey... Did you say something?"

No matter how they strike us at the time, these are not necessarily signals of a lack of care or a lack of desire to address important issues. More than likely, they are signals of one of four significant differences in the way men seem to process and talk about thoughts and emotions—differences largely related to the wiring of the male brain.[5]

Processing Difference 1: Men Often Have to Think Something Through Before They Can Talk It Through

Women tend to be verbal processors—we usually think something through by talking it through. We have lots of connections between the left and right hemispheres of the brain, allowing us to do fast, surface-level processing—and talk about—many thoughts and feelings at the same time.

For example, if I need to figure out how to handle an upsetting situation with the kids, thinking out loud and talking it through with someone helps me deepen and clarify my thoughts. As I circle through the options (probably several times), I get more and more clarity. I also feel better because I have talked through—and thus processed—all those feelings.

For most men, however, that process can be bewildering—and is certainly the polar opposite of their own. Men tend to be internal processors. In most cases (although not all), it is actively difficult for a man to think something through by talking it through. He can *choose* to do so, but the more important or emotionally demanding the issue, the more difficult that becomes. A man's brain is wired to process one thing at a time, going deep within each one, rather than having all the interhemisphere connections that easily juggle many functions at once. So he's more inclined to (a) talk about something, or (b) think about it, or (c) feel something about it. His brain will tackle each task deeply over a period of time, but it won't easily do any of them together. (That is, if it is something requiring any thought. Rhapsodizing on his team's last-second win doesn't count.)

> In most cases, it is actively difficult for a man to think something through by talking it through.

In practice, then, if someone (ahem) presses your husband, son, or boyfriend to talk, that makes it harder for him to think things through. If feelings are swirling around, he'll struggle even more. That's why many men have learned that it usually works far better to get some distance to think about something first.

Let's say *he's* wondering how to handle a tricky situation with the kids. Here's how guys have described it to me: He will think through each option deeply, finish that thought, with all its implications, and then move on to the next one. Then, perhaps, he'll move on to exploring his feelings about the matter. Only when he has processed the issue internally will his brain be able to move on to the next item in line, which is being able to talk about it. And only then will he feel capable of the type of robust and multilayered discussion that is likely to occur when he finally does talk with his mate.

> "I don't know what I'm thinking or feeling yet—but I will once I process it for a while."

I often was skeptical of Jeff's heat-of-the-moment comments such as, "I don't know what I'm thinking" and "I don't know what I'm feeling." *How can you not know what you're thinking or feeling?* I would wonder. But now I realize that he was essentially saying, "I don't know what I'm thinking or feeling *yet*—but I will once I process it for a while."

The truth of this was clear on the second national survey. I asked the men what happened when they'd had a tiff and their wives wanted to talk about it and they didn't. Less than a third said it was because they were simply mad and didn't want to talk. Instead, more than seven out of ten gave answers that fell into the category of needing the space to process it and figure out a solution before they could talk coherently, or so they didn't say something in anger that they'd regret later.

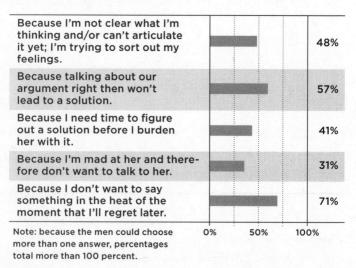

Think about several instances when you've had a tiff with your wife/significant other and she has wanted to talk about it. In a situation where you don't want to talk about it, please check ALL the reasons why. (Choose all correct answers.)

Because I'm not clear what I'm thinking and/or can't articulate it yet; I'm trying to sort out my feelings.	48%
Because talking about our argument right then won't lead to a solution.	57%
Because I need time to figure out a solution before I burden her with it.	41%
Because I'm mad at her and therefore don't want to talk to her.	31%
Because I don't want to say something in the heat of the moment that I'll regret later.	71%

Note: because the men could choose more than one answer, percentages total more than 100 percent.

0%   50%   100%

Thinking to Talk? Or Just to Think?

Now, it is important to note another piece of this truth: if a man is going to actually talk about something important, he has to *know* he's going to talk about it, so he can include that in his processing. As one young man told me,

> I can think something through deeply, in order to decide on the right course of action, and still not be able to articulate it. I can have done the entire internal chess match in my head, and have thought through all the variables, but if I didn't think about needing to *explain* them, I am sometimes totally stumped when my girlfriend asks, "Why?" It's like I did the math problem in my head, not on paper, so I can't show her the steps—even though I actually did do them.

He went on to say that he's fine as long as he knows ahead of time that he'll need to explain why: it simply means that "part of my thinking has to include how to do that."

The Frustrating Reality

Now that you see the male need to think things through first, you can understand how uncomfortable guys must feel when we press them to talk before they've done that, especially when emotions are running high. Consider this back-and-forth exchange between Trevor and Alec, two men I was interviewing together, as they described what happened as emotions began heating up and their wives pressed them to talk about their feelings.

> *Trevor:* She follows me around the house and says, "Why did that upset you? What are you thinking?" And she doesn't realize it'll take me half an hour to work through everything that just happened and figure out what I'm thinking!
>
> *Alec:* Exactly.
>
> Trevor: And then you try and try, and finally you blurt out, "I'm feeling this way."
>
> *Alec:* And then she says, "But why?"
>
> *Trevor* (looking exhausted): It's all I can do to get the *first* level out, and the immediate question "Why?" is *impossible*!
>
> *Alec:* Women interpret that as lacking emotions. It's not lacking them; it's not being able to interpret them. Or articulate them. For women, emotions seem to enhance their ability to articulate clearly with words, but for men, emotions inhibit their ability to articulate.

Combine this reality with the fact that women's brains are simply more wired to talk about things, while men's brains are more geared to act on those things, and there's even more frustration. Men feel just as much inside as we do, but they can't always put those feelings into words right away. In most cases, they can *do* something about their feelings much more easily than they can *talk* about them.

> Men can do something about their feelings much more easily than they can talk about them.

As Jeff and I were driving to pick up our daughter from a remote overnight camp, he likened a man's need to feel prepared for a conversation to my need to have directions for a trip.

Guys don't like to talk through things on the fly. That is not comfortable, because I don't really know where it is going. I like to have a road map of what I've thought through and thus know where the conversation is going. I think for a woman, part of the joy of communication is the discovery. But as a guy, I don't like to discover things in the communication, because I don't trust that it will cover all the nuances I need to think through. So not knowing where the conversation is going creates discomfort, whereas for you, it's part of the adventure.

It's actually the reverse of what happens when we're

driving somewhere. Men don't want to ask for directions, because figuring it out as we go along is where we have that sense of adventure. We love that feeling! Whereas for you, if we were just driving without directions right now, you wouldn't feel real great because you don't know where we're going. That's exactly what it feels like for a guy sometimes when he is unprepared for a conversation.

Processing Difference 2: Men Need Time to Do This

Not surprisingly, the solution for a man to thinking things through is time apart. Men can think and talk about baseball, politics, cooking dinner, chores, or rebuilding the deck with no time delay. But on issues of emotional importance, most men simply need time and space for internal processing. And that may mean a few hours or (for the really big issues) a few days.

While there is no set amount of time that always works (it depends entirely on the guy and the issue), I have heard over and over again that men felt better able to talk about something big the next day. In fact, in his excellent book *What Could He Be Thinking?* Michael Gurian relays what brain scientists have discovered: "Men can take up to *seven hours longer* than women to process complex emotive data." While there are exceptions, Gurian explains, "Men more than women will not know what they feel at the moment of feeling and will take longer to figure it out.

[And] men more than women may not be able to put their feelings into words in the moment and will tend to take longer to express feelings in words than women do."[6]

I'm betting you have seen this seven-hour processing time in practice without knowing what you were seeing. Perhaps you had an argument over dinner, and your man escaped to the gym or the big-screen television in the basement—but the next morning, he was able to talk about it. He wasn't checking out in the way we think *(He doesn't care about me... He's trying to avoid the issue).* Instead he was checking out to get space to do that internal processing.

In most cases, he was probably doing it *because* he cared about you! Here's how one man on the second survey put it: "During a confrontation or argument, I need the cooling period before I can rationally come to an agreement or solution to whatever is wrong. I can't get her to understand that I am not running away from the situation. I have to have some space to gather my thoughts because I might say something that I will regret later... I don't ever want to take a chance of that happening."

> He was probably checking out because he cared about you!

Of course, some men do truly check out, whether out of laziness or to avoid conflict. But in my research that seemed to happen only rarely. Most men care deeply about their wives. From the thousands of stories I've heard, it is clear that we will get a far better outcome and the productive conversation *we* need if we are able to give our men the processing time *they* need.

Processing Difference 3: Men Think Through Everything

Our lack of awareness of this truth is a main reason we have conflict in the first place. It's not that men just need internal processing on those specific things that they decide to think through. It turns out men think everything through. But because they don't do it out loud, it is too easy for us to assume they weren't thinking at all.

> Because men don't think out loud, it is easy for us to assume they weren't thinking at all.

So when our man does something that confounds us, we think (or even say), "What was he thinking!" Well, fess up, girls —the translation of that is "He wasn't thinking." It's synonymous with "Well, that was a boneheaded move, and he did it because he clearly wasn't thinking."

But I discovered that men tend to think through *e-v-e-r-y-t-h-i-n-g*. Including our potential objections to whatever they just did! I was so shocked when I started realizing this that I tested it.

For a whole year, whenever Jeff and I were with another couple and witnessed a situation where the wife was clearly puzzled, or upset with something the husband had done, I would ask permission to jump in (our friends are used to this by now) and ask him about his reasoning. In every single case, the guy relayed a string of well-thought-out decision variables, leaving his wife—and usually me—with our mouths hanging open.

In one such example, Tess watched in horror as her husband, Robert, swiped a dish rag from their sparkling-clean sink and used it to clean mud from his shoes.

Tess: Robert, what on earth are you doing?

Me: Wait! Robert, what were you thinking just now?

Robert: Well, I was thinking that I only had a minute before I had to run to my meeting, that we're out of paper towels in the kitchen, and that this dish rag is getting kind of ratty and it would get the dirt off better than a paper towel anyway. Then I was thinking that I would throw this in the laundry on the way out the door and that it would be a perfect buffing rag for when I wax the car tomorrow.

Tess: Oh.

Now, you and I may or may not agree with Robert's reasoning, but there clearly was reasoning behind a ridiculous-looking action. During this yearlong experiment, not once, when I asked what the man had been thinking, did a guy figuratively scratch his head and answer, "Uh, I dunno." Even if it was a split-second judgment, and even if I personally would not have agreed with it, there was always specific reasoning behind it.

More than eight out of ten men on the second national survey agreed that in such a situation, they likely had thought about things ahead of time, with more than a third saying they had even considered their wives' potential objections!

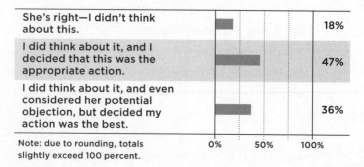

Suppose you are doing some minor project, and it's not something you discussed with your wife/significant other. She gets that "What were you thinking?" look on her face and clearly has a question about what you're doing. Choose the situation that happens most frequently. (Choose one answer.)

She's right—I didn't think about this.	18%
I did think about it, and I decided that this was the appropriate action.	47%
I did think about it, and even considered her potential objection, but decided my action was the best.	36%

Note: due to rounding, totals slightly exceed 100 percent.

0%   50%   100%

As a survey taker put it, "I want her to know that I have often already considered and thought about her potential objections before she voices them."

As you can tell, this ultimately comes back to the respect issue. When confronted by an action that we find inexplicable, do we respect our men, or are we each subconsciously assuming, *That was a boneheaded move, because he wasn't thinking*?

One representative survey taker said the one thing he most wanted his wife to know was, "Sometimes my ideas might not work right, but that doesn't mean I was trying to screw up." He emphasized, "I'm generally trying to do what I think is best for our family."

But Mistakes Are Inevitable

And that brings up a key point: a man's ideas won't always work right any more than ours will. Just because a man thinks something through deeply doesn't mean that his judgment is correct or that he has all the information or experience needed to make a smart decision. (For example, in the dish-rag incident mentioned earlier, how different would it have been if the husband had been unaware that those particular dish towels were the last gift to his wife from her favorite aunt?)

Although many issues are minor ones—on which husbands would love their wives to just trust them—many men emphasized that discussion and even disagreement about important issues is healthy and necessary. We just need to do it with the best assumptions of our mates rather than the worst.

Processing Difference 4: After All That Thinking and Talking, Men Need to Think About Nothing

Sometimes a man isn't stepping back in order to think something deeply through but because he needs time when he doesn't think about anything at all. Many of us have been hurt when, at the end of a long day, we really want to talk about something, and all our husbands want to do is collapse on the couch and surf all 375 channels.

But it turns out that the same brain wiring that requires men to process something deeply before they talk about it also requires mental space to off-load the day's existing inputs before they can take in anymore. Many men described it as feeling like their brain was a sort of container into which stuff poured all day long—and at some point they feel completely full. Doing something completely mindless—such as sitting on the back deck and listening to an iPod, watching television, or even mowing the lawn—allowed some of those things to seep out of their brains and make room for more. Here's how one man put it:

When I get home from work, if my wife tries to talk about the kids or her budget problems at work, it's like she's trying to pour more into an already full bucket. Whatever she's pouring just spills over and I'm not actually taking in what she's saying. But a few years ago we realized that if she can give me just thirty minutes, that is enough for me to let go of some of what is already in the bucket and create enough space for whatever she's wanting to talk about. Sometimes that thirty minutes is torture for her, but she's seen it really does work. So she finally believes that it's not that I'm trying to get away from her.

Working with It, Not Against It

I have seen in my own life—and in researching thousands of couples—that we'll be so much happier when we work *with* the way our men are wired in this area rather than expecting them to have wiring that they simply do not have and getting upset that they don't.

This doesn't mean that men shouldn't make an effort to work with our wiring and those things that are important to us. In *For Men Only,* Jeff and I help male readers understand how women's brains are wired and how to listen in a way that will make us feel cared for. Each of us can adapt and do things that are important for our mates, even when they don't come naturally.

> We'll be so much happier when we work *with* the way our men are wired rather than expecting them to have wiring that they simply do not have.

But since some brain-wiring realities simply don't change, we'll be far happier when, for example, we give them the time they need to process, before expecting them to talk about items of importance. Or give them the mental space to unload full-up brains before expecting them to listen with interest to more.

The best way to learn your man's wiring is to just ask. For example, "When we are in the middle of a conflict and you need time to process it, when do you usually feel able to talk about it? Does that mean a few hours later? the next day?" This has the dual benefit of also validating to him that he's wired differently— and that's okay.

I shared the brain science behind this issue at a recent marriage conference and later overheard two guys talk about how *liberating* the information had been to them. Surprised, I asked Jeff why they might have used that word. He responded,

> Well, this difference in how we process things hits all our insecurities as men. When I'm flustered and I can't talk as well as you can during conflict, I think I'm not as smart as

you are. I can't win in communication with you. And if I can't win, it makes me want to shut down and not even try. So it makes a huge difference for a guy to know "I am smart, I can solve things—I'm just doing it differently than she does." And that will make a guy more willing to engage, because he doesn't feel like a failure. If he knows this is how he is wired, he won't feel stupid anymore.

Dadthink v. Momthink—A Family Story

I was in Colorado speaking at a women's retreat one chilly fall weekend, and I called Jeff on the way to a final dinner. Because of the time difference, it was a couple of hours later at home and Jeff already had put our then six-year-old son to bed. He mentioned offhand that our little boy had wanted to go to bed wearing only his pajama bottoms, so he had let him. I knew Jeff was (like many dads) more inclined to let kids try things, but I couldn't believe Jeff let him go to bed in cold weather without his pajama top! What was he thinking? Didn't he know our little guy would end up freezing and probably wake up crying?

I almost went off on him, then stopped myself. (I know this is lame, but I literally thought to myself, *Respect. Remember the respect chapter.*) I asked, as calmly as I could, "I'm confused. Won't he get cold?"

Jeff chuckled. "Of course. He's been asking to do this the last two nights you've been gone, and I kept telling him, 'You'll be too cold, buddy.' But he kept asking. So I figured, okay, better for him to learn this lesson now than when it is full winter. So I let him do it, but had him sleep in our bed, so when he wakes up because he's too cold, I'll put his top on. And he probably won't want to do that again!"

I instantly was so convicted that I had automatically assumed Jeff didn't know what he was doing—but grateful I had approached it the way I had. And I was determined from then on to make the best assumption rather than the worst.

Recognizing and working with how men process things has eliminated so much unnecessary conflict and made us so much happier in my home, and I'm betting it will do the same in yours.

Five

THE LONELIEST BURDEN

How His Need to Provide Weighs Your Man Down, and Why He Likes It That Way

Even if you made enough income to support the family's lifestyle, it would make no difference to the mental burden your husband feels to provide.

In my interviews I was startled to hear the explicit mental certainty most men had about their roles as family providers. Whatever a man's wife felt about it, whatever she did or didn't earn, he felt that providing was his job. Period. Echoed by many, one man stated it this way: "I love my wife, but I can't depend on her to provide. That's my job."

In several interviews, the man's wife was sitting right next to him. One wife, shocked, turned to her husband and said, "But I've always worked! I've always contributed to the family budget!"

His gentle response: "You working or not is irrelevant. Not to the family budget—it does ease some of the financial pressure. But it is irrelevant to my need to provide."

"IT'S MY JOB"

We have all heard that men want to be providers. Each man wants to club the buffalo over the head and drag it back to the cave to his woman. But what few women understand is that this is not just an issue of "wanting to." Rather, it is a burden that presses heavily on men and won't let up.

Consider the stunning results from the survey: a man's need to provide goes so deep that even if you did bring home enough money to nicely support the whole family, your man would probably still feel compelled to provide.

Suppose your wife/significant other earned enough to support your family's lifestyle. Would you still feel a compulsion to provide for your family? (Choose one answer.)

Yes	78%
No	22%

0%   50%   100%

It didn't matter whether the men were married or single, religious or not, old or young—nearly eight in ten felt this compulsion. The only major difference was an ethnic one: the compulsion was stronger among minority groups.

> For most men, the drive to provide is so deeply rooted that almost nothing can relieve them of their sense of duty.

Does the big picture here surprise you as much as it did me? Popular culture often portrays men as willing freeloaders. What they really want to do, we're told, is park on the recliner and command the remote. But in reality, for most men the drive to provide is so deeply rooted that almost nothing can relieve them of their sense of duty. It appears to be nothing less than an obsession—similar in some ways to women's obsessive body insecurity ("I wish I could lose weight!").

"And It's My Job All the Time!"

The second thing the survey revealed is that men don't merely carry this burden; they carry it constantly. There's no respite—the knowledge of their responsibility is always there, pressing down on them. Look at the data:

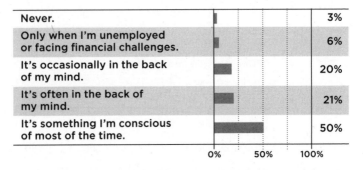

Under what circumstances do you think about your responsibility to provide for your family? (Choose one answer.)

Never.	3%
Only when I'm unemployed or facing financial challenges.	6%
It's occasionally in the back of my mind.	20%
It's often in the back of my mind.	21%
It's something I'm conscious of most of the time.	50%

0%   50%   100%

Stop for a second and read those results slowly, until they sink in. A large majority of men (71 percent) say that their responsibility to provide is always or often on their minds. Think about what it must feel like to be conscious of this burden most of the time!

An employee at my local Costco described the provider impulse this way: "It's always in the back of my mind that I need to provide. A man won't feel like a man if he doesn't."

"Is it ever *not* in the back of your mind?" I asked.

"Nope," he declared. "If you're going to be the man, that's just the way it is."

THE INNER LIFE OF A PROVIDER

What drives this compulsion to provide? And since this need appears to be unchanging—despite our modern dual-income culture in which a wife can often provide for herself, thank you very much—what must we learn to recognize and (for the most part) accept about the way our men are wired?

Providing Is at the Core of a Man's Identity

Being a provider appears to be at the core of a man's identity as a male and as a person of worth: he feels that to be a man, he needs to be a provider. Even single men feel this way. On one long plane trip, I asked the unmarried man sitting next to me whether he felt a burden to provide even though he had no one to provide for. "It's still the same," he said. "You want to be in control of your life." He explained that if he didn't provide for himself, other people would have to, and he would no longer be in control.

> Men feel powerful when they provide. And they want to be depended on.

In other words, being the provider isn't just a burden but a highly desirable goal. Men feel powerful when they provide. And they want to be depended on. The ability to take care of those they feel responsible for lies at the very center of their sense of personal significance. Providing for those he loves is not just what a man does for a living—in a unique way, it is an enormous part of who he is.

I was telling one man how surprised I was at how intense guys are about being the providers. "Maybe you should see this as the flip side of how we think about sex," he offered. "About sex, men are pretty utilitarian and women are emotional. About money, work, or providing, women are utilitarian, but men get emotional!"

Providing Is a Primary Way to Say "I Love You"

For a man, bringing home a paycheck is love talk, pure and simple. He has something to prove ("I can take care of you, I am worthy of you"), and he wants to deliver.

Even more pointedly, in a man's mind, providing for his wife is a central way of expressing his love. As one young man told me, "My job is to worry about providing so that my wife doesn't have to. That's one way I show her I love her."

It's ironic that we may complain about our man's work habits, not realizing that he thinks he is saying "I love you"—and we are complaining about it! This dynamic is both confusing and distressing for men.

A couple we know had recently read *The Lights of Tenth Street,* in which the main male character frequently travels and his wife at one point wonders whether he cares more about work than her. After reading this scene, our male friend—who also travels a lot—turned to his wife and asked, "Do *you* ever wonder that?"

Surprised, she answered, "Well, of course!"

Flabbergasted, he said, "Why do you think I do work this much? It's *because* I care about you!" He had been traveling for almost twenty-five years, and his wife had never understood that he viewed it as a sacrifice he made out of love and a desire to provide for her.

> "Why do you think I do work this much? It's *because* I care about you!"

Providing Accompanies His Need to Succeed

Now, let's be honest—other motivations are also at work here. Many of the men I interviewed combined a selfless desire to provide with a powerful internal drive to succeed and find pleasure in their work. Half of the men surveyed agreed that if they worked a lot, it was because they felt, "I've got to work a lot to get ahead, and I want to get ahead" or "I want to be working this much because I enjoy work" or both.

On the survey, one man echoed the feelings of many men I interviewed. He said the one thing he wished his wife knew was "that I enjoy my career and that being successful is important for me and for us."

Just as women can have multiple reasons for doing the things we value, including work, so men do too. We should appreciate our mates' drive to work, provide, and succeed as long as they maintain some balance and the home relationships remain strong. In particular, we should be grateful if our mates are in the enviable position of loving what they do for a living.

Providing Carries an Ongoing Risk of Failure

Now let's make the connection between the provider impulse and an earlier topic—your man's deep insecurity that he may not cut it. It turns out that providing is *the* key arena where men experience the ongoing risk of failure.

Paul of Tarsus said that the man who doesn't provide for his family is "worse than an infidel." As a woman, I always assumed that was a command: "Provide for your family or you are worse than an infidel." What I didn't realize was that, although it may in fact be a command, it is also a description of how terrible men feel about themselves when times are tight and they are not doing a good job of providing.

Most men, as you now see, don't need that command. They are driven to provide no matter what. That statement could just as easily be read as a reflection of internal angst—the horrible feeling that one is truly "worse than an infidel."

"I Feel like My Skin Is Being Flayed Off"

Because of this dynamic, men constantly worry about failure at work, layoffs, or a downturn in business. Since a majority of men (61 percent) said they regularly felt unappreciated at work, it appears that many truly think they are at risk. But because we see our men as talented and effective, we may not understand this fear and therefore may not realize how strongly they feel about doing whatever is necessary to protect their jobs and provide for their families.

If the worst happens and the family encounters financial problems, your man feels like a failure. Even if the financial problems have nothing to do with him (say, for example, his biggest client went out of business), if the result is that you have to adjust your lifestyle, can't buy the children the birthday presents they asked for, or have trouble paying the mortgage, he suffers emotional torture.

One man, whose business is currently in a very difficult season, described it this way: "Every day, with every step I take, I feel like my skin is being flayed off."

Even without financial problems, men can still wrestle with a feeling of failure if they aren't bringing in most of the family income. An increasing number of men earn less than their wives or have become the primary caregivers for children. These men told me that even when it was a logical, mutual decision made with their wives, they still struggled at times. In some ways, they said, they had even *more* of a need to be respected and appreciated as providing—whether that meant being a great dad or covering an important share of the bills.

> If the family encounters financial problems, and you have to adjust your lifestyle, your man feels like a failure.

Providers Can Feel Trapped

Every day, providers can feel a strange tension between wanting to be depended on and feeling trapped by that responsibility. The vast majority of men who put in long hours do so not just because they want to get ahead but because they believe, as several men told me, "there is no other option." And they get frustrated when we don't understand that, particularly when they feel *we* are the source of some of the pressure.

For a man, today's version of dragging the buffalo home isn't just meeting the minimum bills. It's also about making his wife happy by giving her the things she wants. And without realizing it, we may send signals that we care more about the things than about how hard our men have to work to provide them.

One very direct survey response made me wince. This man wished he could tell his wife, "I feel confused. You want me home more (I travel each week and really wish I could be home), yet you want a new house, nice things, substantial income, etc. Please understand the Catch-22 I am in. Due to past cutbacks with previous employers, I had to take this job. I feel like I am pushing two big rocks uphill."

Because they want to make us happy, men are surprisingly sensitive to hearing pressure from us where none was intended. One man shared, "Yesterday my wife was annoyed at some stubborn old stains and said, 'I really don't like this carpet.' I felt so bad. Like I was failing her, that I wasn't able to give her the new carpet she wanted." He was shocked when I told him his wife was likely simply venting rather than stating her displeasure with his ability to provide.

Even without creating financial pressure, we can also inadvertently pressure our men in other ways, such as by complaining about their long work hours. Many of us secretly suspect that if our men would just tell their bosses no once in a while, they would be able to spend more time with us. Or we may worry that our men just don't want to be with us very much. So, on the survey, I just *had* to test these suspicions. You know how many men were actually thinking one of those two things? A tiny fraction (5 percent or less).

Instead, the vast majority (82 percent) had what I would characterize as an unselfish motivation, answering that if they didn't work that hard, they would let their families and/or the organizations down. Most of these men answered, "If I don't work this hard, I feel like my job might be at risk, and I do have to provide for my family" or "There is no way to support our family lifestyle without working this hard—I guess I could find a job with fewer hours, but it wouldn't pay enough." Furthermore, half of those men went out of their way to add that they didn't want to be away from their families so much.

Consider the response of one surveyed man, whose mate had probably challenged him about his priorities: "My priorities *are* my family. I wish I knew of some way not to work so much, or to be available more, but I don't know how to make this work otherwise. I wish she was more aware of this."

Don't get me wrong—I am the last person to advise sitting in silence if you're concerned about your man's time away from family. I tend to go too far in the other direction! But if you can put yourself in your husband's shoes and understand how he might feel trapped, he's more likely to see your concern as supportive rather than antagonistic.

Providing Means Earning Enough for Both Present and Future

For men, the need to provide for today is amplified by anxieties about also providing for the future. Essentially, they feel like they have to earn two incomes. One man wrote, "I wish my wife would understand that I am not only providing for the present, but I am trying to save for our golden years."

Many working men also mentioned anxiety at the idea of retirement's emotional consequences. They said that when a man gets a social security or pension check without feeling like he is earning it, he feels like he has lost his purpose.

This dynamic may partly explain why men who are unemployed or on welfare so often get depressed and lose motivation. They feel like they have failed at being a provider, and are less than a man.

SO HOW DO WE RESPOND?

Now that we grasp how overwhelming the provider impulse is, what should we do about it?

Reconsider Existing Areas of Conflict

Ladies, we must face the fact that our mates feel caught, with few options, on provider issues. And they probably also feel deeply misunderstood by us. We need to take a look at where both facts may have impacted our relationships.

For example, once I understood Jeff's provider burden, I suddenly grasped that an unwillingness to stand up to his boss wasn't some uncharacteristic weakness but a strong desire to continue to be able to pay the mortgage. Which meant that my primary response should be appreciation more than criticism.

> We must face the fact that our mates feel caught, with few options, on provider issues.

Some women might suddenly realize the pressure they have inadvertently been putting on their husbands by coming home with new shopping bags every day—while others may grasp just how painful it is for their husbands to earn less than they do. Others may understand what one man described as "the stress of feeling that you are asking him to choose between one huge need (to provide financial security for you) and another (to show you he really does care about family time)."

Of course, just because we understand a man's viewpoint doesn't mean that we will always agree with it. But regardless, understanding where your man is coming from is essential to any kind of productive conversation.

Help Relieve the Pressure

Many of us have faced difficult financial seasons in recent years, and obviously that's hard for everybody. It is easy to get nervous and blame our husbands or pressure them to "do something." But most men don't need more pressure. They've got that in spades internally, and when we add to it, we're probably demotivating them instead of helping.

What they need instead is our steadfast belief that they will solve the problem ("I know you can do it") and our steadfast offer to help them do what it takes to stay afloat. That may mean showing our willingness to bring in more income ourselves or expressing excitement about staying with friends at the beach in the off-season instead of going on that romantic Caribbean vacation. (I say *excitement* rather than *willingness* because a man will internalize your disappointment as a personal failure to provide.)

> During difficult financial seasons, they need our steadfast belief that they will solve the problem.

Several men have told me that the best thing their mate can do is to show that she realizes how tight things are by refusing to spend money unnecessarily. That, combined with our emotional support, does wonders for the man's feeling that "we can get through this."

But how can we be emotionally supportive when *we* need support? Having gone through an extremely difficult financial season ourselves, I can say that the answer is to cast our cares for provision on the Lord rather than on our men. In the end, it is His job to carry the burden.

In the conclusion to the Lord of the Rings movie trilogy, when the hero is completely exhausted from carrying his terrible burden, his best friend lifts him to his shoulders, crying, "I can't carry it for you…but I can carry you!"[7] By praying for our husbands and looking to the Lord rather than to our circumstances, we trust Him to carry both our husbands and their burdens. Then from the overflow of our hearts, we can give back to and encourage our men.

Encourage and Appreciate Him

One man gave a great summation of what a man needs most, whether a couple is "in plenty or in want": "Thank him regularly for providing. He forgets quickly."

Most of us want to support our men, and in this case being a support means understanding them, appreciating them, and helping to relieve the pressure they feel rather than adding to it.

Being a support means helping to relieve the pressure they feel rather than adding to it.

One husband put it this way: "Make sure he knows your pleasure in any financial progress so he knows all his obsessive hard work was worth it. And when he comes in really late from an extra-long day at the office, surprise him with a thank-you gift. Use your imagination."

Six

SEX CHANGES EVERYTHING

Why Sex Unlocks a Man's Emotions (Guess Who Holds the Key?)

Your sexual desire for your husband profoundly affects his sense of well-being and confidence in all areas of his life.

It's not exactly a shocker to say that men want more sex. We've known that—and giggled about it with our girlfriends—since junior high. But do you know how strongly your man feels this need? And more to the point, *why*?

On each survey and in my random interviews around the country, an urgent theme emerged: Men want more sex than they are getting. And what's more, they believe that the women who love them don't seem to realize that this is a crisis—not only for the man, but for the relationship.

Why on earth is it a crisis? After all, a lot of other legitimate needs get in the way. Like sleep. Isn't sex just a biological urge that he really should be able to do without? Well...no. For your husband, sex is more than just a physical need. Lack of sex is as emotionally serious to him as, say, his sudden silence would be to you, were he simply to stop communicating with you. It is just as wounding to him, just as much a legitimate grievance—and just as dangerous to your marriage.

SEX FILLS A POWERFUL EMOTIONAL NEED

Although popular opinion portrays males as one giant sex gland with no emotions attached, that is the furthest thing from the truth. But because men don't tend to describe their sexual needs in emotional terms, we women may not realize that.

In a very deep way, your man often feels isolated and burdened by secret feelings of inadequacy. Making love with you assures him that you find him desirable, salves a deep sense of loneliness, and gives him the strength and well-being necessary to face the world with confidence. And, of course, sex also makes him feel loved—in fact, he can't feel completely loved without it.

At the most basic level, your man wants to be wanted. Look

at the overwhelming response from the second nationally representative survey.

With regard to sex, for some men it is sufficient to be sexually gratified whenever they want. For other men it is also important to feel wanted and desired by their wife. How important is it to you to also feel sexually wanted and desired by your wife? (Choose one answer.)

Very important	66%
Somewhat important	31%
Not very important, as long as I get enough sex	2%
Irrelevant, as long as I get enough sex	<1%

This topic earned the highest degree of unanimity of any question: 97 percent of men said getting enough sex wasn't, by itself, enough—they wanted to feel wanted.

> At the most basic level, your man wants to be wanted.

One man I interviewed summed it up like this: "Everyone thinks women are more emotional than men. And everyone thinks that when it comes to sex, guys just want to 'do it' and women are more into the emotion and cuddling of it. So women think there are no emotions there. But there *are,* and when you say no, you are messing with all those emotions."

And it's not only a flat no that hurts. The survey showed that even if they were getting all the sex they wanted, three out of four men would still feel empty if their wives weren't both engaged and satisfied.

Imagine that your wife offers all the sex that you want but does it reluctantly or simply to accommodate your sexual needs. Will you be sexually satisfied? (Choose one answer.)

Yes	26%
No	74%

0%　　　50%　　　100%

As one survey taker explained, "I think that my wife, after twentysome years of marriage, knows how important my need for sex is, but I wish she knew how important it is to me that she *needs* me sexually. She probably does not need sex so much, but I need her to want and need sex with me."

Reality Check!

I believe that most of us aren't manipulatively withholding something we know is critical to our husbands' sense of well-being.

Much more likely is that, after a long day at the office or with the kids, we just don't feel an overwhelming desire to rip off our husbands' clothes and go at it. I suspect we simply don't realize the emotional consequences of our responses (or lack of them) and view their desire for sex more as a physical desire or even an insensitive demand. Once we truly comprehend the truth behind our husbands' advances, we're more likely to *want* to respond.

WHY IS SEX SO IMPORTANT?

What kinds of emotional needs does your sexual interest meet for your man? In the written survey comments and in my interviews, I noticed two parallel trends—the great benefits a fulfilling sex life creates in a man's inner life and, conversely, the wounds created when lovemaking is reluctant or lacking.

Benefit 1: Fulfilling Sex Makes Him Feel Loved and Desired

Not surprisingly, the first thing that surfaced from the survey comments was that having a regular, mutually enjoyed sex life was critical to the man's feeling of being loved and desired. One plea captured it perfectly:

> I wish that my wife understood that making a priority
> of meeting my intimacy needs is the loudest and clearest

way she can say, "You are more important to me than anything else in the world." It is a form of communication that speaks more forcefully, with less room for misinterpretation, than any other.

The reason why this message is needed is that many men, even those with close friendships, seem to live with a deep sense of loneliness that is quite foreign to us oh-so-relational women. And making love is the purest salve for that loneliness.

One man told me, "I feel like I go out into the ring every day and fight the fight. It's very lonely. That's why, when the bell rings, I want my wife to be there for me."

Another related that sentiment to the power of fulfilling sex. "A man really does feel isolated, even with his wife. But in making love, there is one other person in this world that you can be completely vulnerable with and be totally accepted and not judged. It is a solace that goes very deep into the heart of a man."

"Making love is a solace that goes very deep into the heart of a man."

Benefit 2: Fulfilling Sex Gives Him Confidence

Your desire for him goes beyond making him feel wanted and loved. As we touched on in the impostor chapter, your desire is a bedrock form of support that gives him power to face the rest of his daily life with a sense of confidence and well-being.

A few years back there were a series of television commercials for Viagra in which a man's colleagues and friends repeatedly stop him and ask what's different about him. New haircut? Been working out? Promotion? Nope, the man tells them all with a little smile.

One man I interviewed brought up those ads. "Every man immediately understands what that commercial is saying—it's all about guys feeling good about themselves. The ad portrays a truth that all men intuitively recognize. They are more confident and alive when their sex life is working."

On the survey, again, three out of four men agreed.

Imagine that your wife was an interested and motivated sexual partner, and you therefore had an active love life. How would having sex with her as often as you wanted affect your emotional state? (Choose one answer.)

It would have little or no effect—sex seems unrelated to my emotions or how I feel about the rest of my life.	23%
It would have a positive effect—it would give me a greater sense of well-being and satisfaction with life.	77%

0% 50% 100%

Once my eyes were opened to this truth, I realized how often I'd heard the "man code" for this fact but failed to understand it. When men had told me they felt better when they got more sex, I had just assumed they meant physically better. But as one husband told me, "What happens in the bedroom really does affect how I feel the next day at the office." Another wrote, "Sex is a release of day-to-day pressures…and *seems to make everything else better*" (emphasis mine).

Once we see how central a man's sex life is to his emotional well-being, we need to know what happens in his heart when he doesn't get what he's looking for.

> "What happens in the bedroom really does affect how I feel the next day at the office."

Wound 1: "If She Doesn't Want to, I Feel Incredible Rejection"

As much as men want sex, most of them would rather go out and clip the hedges in the freezing rain than make love with a wife who appears to be responding out of duty. My husband, Jeff, explained: "The guy isn't going to be rejected by the hedges. And that's the issue. If she's just responding because she has to, he's being rejected by his wife."

Again, keeping in mind that what he wants most is for you to desire him, try to see this rejection issue from the man's point of view. If you agree, but don't make an effort to get really engaged with the man you love, he hears you saying, "You're incapable of turning me on even when you try, and I really don't care about what matters deeply to you." On the other hand, if you don't agree at all, but throw out the classic "Not tonight, dear," he hears, "You're so undesirable that you can't compete with my pillow...and I really don't care about what matters deeply to you."

Although you might just be saying you don't want sex at that point in time, he hears the much more painful message that you don't want *him*. Here's what the men themselves said on the survey:

- "She doesn't understand that I feel loved by sexual caressing, and if she doesn't want to, I feel incredible rejection."
- "When she says no, I feel that I am REJECTED. 'No' is *not* no to sex—as she might feel. It is no to me as I am. And I am vulnerable as I ask or initiate. It's plain and simple rejection."

"'No' is *not* no to sex—as she might feel. It is no to me as I am."

- "She doesn't understand how even her occasional dismissals make me feel less desirable. I can't resist her. I wish that I, too, were irresistible. She says I am. But her ability to say no so easily makes it hard to believe."

This feeling of personal rejection, and a sense that his wife doesn't really desire him, tends to lead a man into darker waters.

Wound 2: Your Lack of Desire Can Send Him into Depression

If your sexual desire gives your husband a sense of well-being and confidence, you can understand why an ongoing perception that you don't desire him would translate into a nagging lack of confidence, withdrawal, and depression.

The men I talked to scoffed at my tentative suggestion that a string of similar rejections wouldn't necessarily mean that their wives were rejecting them as men. They warned that any woman sending those signals would undermine the loving environment she wants most because, as one man said, "She is going to have one depressed man on her hands."

A man can't just turn off the physical and emotional importance of sex, which is why its lack can be compared to the emotional pain you'd feel if your husband simply stopped talking to you. Consider the painful words of this truly deprived husband—words that other men, upon reading them, call "heartbreaking":

We've been married for a long time. I deeply regret and resent the lack of intimacy of nearly any kind for the duration of our marriage. I feel rejected, ineligible, insignificant, lonely, isolated, and abandoned as a result. Not having the interaction I anticipated prior to marriage is like a treasure lost and irretrievable. It causes deep resentment and hurt within me. This in turn fosters anger and feelings of alienation.

HOW CAN WE OVERCOME THE "SEX GAP"?

I can't tell you how often I heard a man's not-at-all-veiled appeal for his wife to not only desire him but to do something about it. Although every intimate relationship has its own story, here are a few ways to begin.

Choose to Love Him in the Way He Needs

Okay, if you're like me, you've probably been viewing your man's sexual need as mostly physical—important, yes, but probably also optional. By comparison, when you've been tugged on by little hands all day, your need for sleep can seem both important and immediately necessary. But once you realize that your man is actually saying, "This is essential to my feeling of being loved and desired by you, and is critical to counteract my stress, my fears, and my loneliness," well…that suddenly puts it in a different category. So how might you respond?

First, know that you're responding to a tender heart hiding behind all that testosterone. If at all possible, respond to his advances with your full emotional involvement, knowing that you're touching his *heart*. But if responding physically seems out of the question, let your words be heart words—reassuring, affirming, adoring. Do everything in your power—using words and actions your husband understands—to keep those pangs of personal rejection from striking the man you love. Leave him in no doubt that you love to love him.

And second, remember that if you do respond physically but do it just to meet his needs without getting engaged, you're not actually meeting his needs. In fact, you might as well send him out to clip the hedges. So enjoy God's intimate gift, and make the most of it!

> Know that you're responding to a tender heart hiding behind all that testosterone.

Get Involved…and Have More Fun Too

One man on the churchgoers' survey was particularly blunt: "The woman needs to play an active role in the sex life. She needs to tell her mate what she needs, wants, and feels. Passive wife = boring life."

Whew!

I discovered that many men love the secret knowledge of having a wife who is sexually motivated. A few years ago, I overheard a thirty-year-old single friend telling Jeff what he wanted in a wife. "I want a wife who is a model of Christian virtue—godly, faithful, and always kind to others." A grin crept into his voice. "But when I get her home…!"

"It's like that song 'Behind Closed Doors' from the seventies," a married friend told me recently. "That's what every man wants—the girl next-door in the living room and a wildcat in the bedroom."[8]

> Some of us may think that being a "wildcat"
> is a bit beyond us. Not so, say the men.

Now, some of us may laugh at that and think that being a "wildcat" is a bit beyond us. Not so, say the men. All that means, they say, is a wife who makes the first move once in a while and who brings all her attentions and passion for her man to bed with her. Do that, and watch your husband light up with delight!

If You Need Help, Get It

I recognize that some women might wish that they *could* respond more wholeheartedly to their husbands' sexual needs but feel stopped in their tracks for various personal reasons. I don't want to add any more frustration. I do, however, want to encourage you to get the personal or professional help you need to move forward. The choice to pursue healing will be worth it, both for you and for the man you love.

Make Sex a Priority

An excerpt from a *Today's Christian Woman* article by Jill Eggleton Brett captures this issue—and provides an important challenge to change our thinking. The author starts by admitting that, although her husband really wanted to make love more often, it "just wasn't one of my priorities." She then describes a subsequent revelation:

> I felt what I did all day was meet other people's needs. Whether it was caring for my children, working in ministry, or washing my husband's clothes, by the end of the day I wanted to be done need-meeting. I wanted my pillow and a magazine. But God prompted me: *Are the "needs" you meet for your husband the needs he wants met?* If our daughters weren't perfectly primped, he didn't complain. If the kitchen floor needed mopping, he didn't say a word. And if he didn't have any socks to wear, he simply threw them in the washer himself. I soon realized I regularly said "no" to the one thing he asked of me.

I sure wasn't making myself available to my husband by militantly adhering to my plan for the day.... Would the world end if I didn't get my tires rotated? I'd been so focused on what I wanted to get done and what my children needed, I'd cut my hubby out of the picture.[9]

"I realized I regularly said 'no' to the one thing he asked of me."

Are the many other things that take our time and energy truly as important as this one? Now would be a good time to re-evaluate priorities with the help of our husbands so they know that we are taking this seriously.

Getting Those "Love Signals" Right

In closing, I thought it would be encouraging to look in on how one average husband and wife handled this issue. Mark and Anne had a good marriage in general. They had been married fifteen years when Mark noticed their sex life starting to wane. Anne was not responding the way she used to, was just not as interested, too busy, too tired. They didn't stop making love, but as Mark says, "It just seemed to be less of a priority for her."

Mark is a businessman, and he sometimes works long hours, which used to be a source of grief for Anne. Years earlier, she had sat down with him and explained that it wasn't so much the hours that hurt her but that he didn't come home when he said he would. She told him that he was a great husband, but that this one thing made her feel very uncared for. She told him that his willingness to tell her a realistic time when he'd be home and stick to it was—for her—one of the most important signals of his love. Mark understood and that became a top priority for him.

Now, years later, Mark sat down with Anne and told her that he was concerned about the drop-off in their sex life. He drew a parallel to Anne's need for him to be home when promised. He said, "I could be a great husband but not do this one thing that is really important to you, and I'd still fail at making you feel loved. Having sex like we used to, having you be responsive to me, is the same thing for me."

Anne had never understood it that way, and it was important for her to hear that she could be a great wife, but if she didn't respond to his need to feel desired—one of his most important "love signals"—she'd still fail at making him feel loved. As Mark now says, "It clicked for her. And that changed everything."

Has your husband been sending you signals?

Has your husband been sending you signals that he is unhappy about your responsiveness to him? It's possible that he may wish he could explain this to you but doesn't know how. Or maybe he's tried but you've discounted the importance of his request.

Having heard from so many men on this, I would urge you: Don't discount it. It is more important to him—and to your relationship and therefore your own joy in marriage—than you can imagine.

Now that you understand the tender places in your husband's heart, hopefully you have developed compassion for him and the way he is wired. Let's take that compassion and understanding with us as we examine the next area of his inner life.

Seven

KEEPER OF THE PHOTO FILES

Why It's So Difficult for Him Not to Look, and So Hard to Forget What He's Seen

Even happily married men struggle with being pulled toward live and recollected images of other women.

S*cene One:* Doug, a successful businessman with a wife and kids, has traveled to California for a business deal. The conference room fills with top executives, each one planning on giving him a presentation. The first executive, an attractive woman, walks to the whiteboard. She has a great figure, Doug notices, and her well-fitted suit shows it off tastefully. As she begins her presentation, the woman is friendly but all business.

Scene Two: I'm talking to a series of randomly selected Christian men who are serious about their faith and (if they're married) genuinely devoted to their wives. I describe scene one above and tell them it is straight out of my novel *The Lights of Tenth Street.* Then I ask each man a question: "If you were Doug, what would be going through your mind as the female executive makes her presentation?" Here are some of their answers:

- "Great body... Stop it! What am I thinking?"
- "I feel an instant tightening in my gut."
- "I bet she's using those curves to sell this deal."
- "Look at her face, look at her face, look at her face..."
- "It is hard for me to concentrate on her presentation because I'm trying so hard to look at her face and not her body."
- "I have to be ruthless about pushing back these images—and they keep intruding."
- "I wonder what's under that nice suit. Stop it! Concentrate on the presentation."

If you had been with me, listening to those men, what would you be thinking? I confess that their answers both amazed and dismayed me. Yet as I heard men I trusted reveal similar reactions over and over, I realized that this temptation must be normal. (And for this chapter in particular, remember that by "normal" I do not necessarily mean "easy to accept" or "what you would prefer" or even "right.")

Although I'd always heard that men are visual, I had never understood what that actually meant.

WHAT "MEN ARE VISUAL" MEANS

Here's the insight I stumbled on by accident, and which applies to even the most faithful of husbands: Regardless of whether they let this temptation into their thoughts (and many men work hard to avoid doing so), the unique wiring of the male brain creates an instinctive pull to visually consume the image of an attractive woman—and these images can be just as alluring whether they are live or recollected. Two areas of this "men are visual" thing surfaced that I, at least, didn't really get before:

- First, a woman who is dressed to show off a great body is an eye magnet that is incredibly difficult to avoid, and even if a man forces himself to not look, he is acutely aware of that woman's presence.

- Second, even when no such eye magnet is present, each man has a mental photo file of stored images that can intrude into his thoughts without warning, or be called up at will.

As I'll explain shortly, both are related to a type of brain wiring that is almost universal among men. Some women have this wiring too—and if you are one who does, these revelations may not seem surprising. But for the rest of us, it may seem a mystery—or worse. We might even experience it as a personal failure on our part (for not being enough of a woman to keep our man's attention) or as a personal betrayal on his (why would a loving and committed husband have to push back images of other women at all?).

Thankfully, as we delve deeper, discovering how hard-wired this compulsion and temptation is—and how little it has to do with us—puts those concerns in the right perspective and helps us support our men (including our sons) in this culture.

This book doesn't allow space to delve into a serious visually related issue like pornography addiction. Thankfully, many excellent resources do offer specialized help (several are listed at for womenonlybook.com). In the meantime, let's look at what every woman should know about the visual wiring of men.

The Visual Wiring of the Male Brain

I have found that understanding the basics of brain science has been extremely helpful.[10] A man's brain structure and chemical mix wire him to be extremely visually oriented. That wiring makes him more likely to perceive attractive images as sexual, and triggers an initial reaction that is both instinctive and automatic. From there he can choose—if he opts to apply his willpower—how he will think and behave.

The most important wiring to understand is a small center

of the brain called the nucleus accumbens. It resides in the back of the brain—the area that controls stuff you don't consciously think about, like digestion and breathing. The nucleus accumbens is the part of the brain that automatically lights up when, for example, you are extremely hungry and you walk into a room to see a buffet of yummy-looking food. First, your brain draws you toward that food in a gut-level, automatic way. But then the cortical (thinking) centers in your brain kick in. Your ability to exercise your willpower kicks in. You might decide to start eating, or—thinking perhaps about your pocketbook, your schedule, or your waistline—you might force your thoughts (and your eyes) away.

Clinical studies show the same process happening in a man's brain when he sees an attractive woman dressed to call attention to a good figure (such as showing cleavage or wearing a tight skirt). The nucleus accumbens in his brain lights up, and he will most likely experience a primal, physical temptation to visually consume that image. But then his thoughts (and his will) kick in, and he can decide whether to continue to entertain that image or to wrench his thoughts away.

Most women don't understand this sequence because, on visual-sexual matters, our brains respond quite differently. In most cases, when we see an attractive man, our nucleus accumbens stays dark and instead our cortical centers light up. So we *think* to ourselves, "Wow, he's an attractive man." Since ours is a thinking-oriented response from the beginning, most of us simply have no idea what a man's initial, reflexive response feels like—or even that it exists.

Actually, brain scientists note two separate but related compulsions stemming from male brain wiring that greatly impact men in today's culture. Let's keep an open mind and look at them together.

Compulsion 1: A Man Can't Not Notice

In the survey, we created a scene similar to Doug's and asked men to predict their responses. Consider the results:

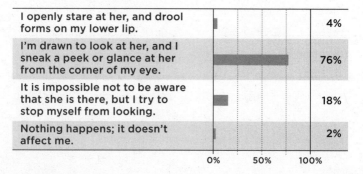

Imagine you are sitting alone in a train station and a woman with a great body walks in and stands in a nearby line. What is your reaction to the woman? (Choose one answer.)

I openly stare at her, and drool forms on my lower lip.	4%
I'm drawn to look at her, and I sneak a peek or glance at her from the corner of my eye.	76%
It is impossible not to be aware that she is there, but I try to stop myself from looking.	18%
Nothing happens; it doesn't affect me.	2%

0%   50%   100%

The first fact is that a whopping 98 percent of men put their response to an eye-catching woman in "can't *not* notice" categories (only 2 percent were unaffected by a woman with a great body). And the results were essentially the same among happily married and devoted Christian men—since they still had male brains.

Many men explained the power of this desire to look, even when they tried *not* to or when the attractive woman in question left their line of sight. One husband with a happy twenty-year marriage described a typical scenario: "My wife and I recently went out to dinner at a nice restaurant with some friends. The hostess was extremely attractive and was wearing formfitting clothes that showed off a great figure. For the rest of the night, it was impossible not to be aware that she was across the restaurant, walking around. Our group had a great time with our lovely wives, but I guarantee you that our wives didn't know that every man at that table was acutely aware of that woman's presence and was doing his utmost not to look in that direction."

In other words, the nucleus accumbens of the male brain had lit up, the biological impulse to visually consume that image had been triggered, and all the men were exerting their will to force their thoughts and their eyes away.

Of course, as you can tell from the survey, some men in that situation would sneak a peek instead. Even faithful, godly husbands who usually tried not to do that described sometimes giving in to an almost overwhelming curiosity. One faithful husband whom I highly trust confessed, "If I see a woman with a great body walk into Home Depot and I close my eyes or turn away until she passes, for the next half hour, I'm keenly aware that she's in there somewhere. I'm ashamed to say that, more than once, I've gone looking down the aisles, hoping to catch a glimpse."

Now think back to the very opening of this book. These examples clarify why Jeff would suddenly turn his head as we walked the streets of New York: He was choosing to honor me. He had just seen an attractive woman and was forcing himself to look away so the image would not linger.

And that brings us to the second fact.

Compulsion 2: A Man Has a Mental Photo File of Sensual Images

We've all heard that the male half of the population thinks about sex a lot. What I didn't realize was that they aren't exactly thinking about sex (as in, *I wonder if my wife will be in the mood tonight?*). Rather, they're picturing it, or picturing a sexual image. And those pictures aren't, unfortunately, always of their wives. They are often images that have been involuntarily burned in their brains just by living in today's culture—images that can arise without warning.

You might be wondering, *What kinds of images?*

Apparently just about anything: the memory of an intimate

time with you (good) or a memory from a *Playboy* magazine (bad). It could be a recollection of the shapely woman who walked through the parking lot two minutes ago or something he saw in a movie two years ago. As a result of his neural wiring, these images often arise in his brain without warning—even if the guy doesn't want them there. Or specific images can be recalled on purpose. As several men put it, "I have an unending supply of images in my head, stretching back to my teens."

> Images often arise without warning, even if the guy doesn't want them.

The survey results were clear:

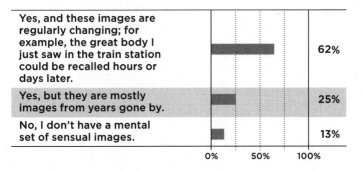

Many men have a mental set of sensual images that rise up or can be conjured up in their minds. Does this apply to you? (Choose one answer.)

Yes, and these images are regularly changing; for example, the great body I just saw in the train station could be recalled hours or days later.	62%
Yes, but they are mostly images from years gone by.	25%
No, I don't have a mental set of sensual images.	13%

0%   50%   100%

In total, 87 percent of men say these images pop up in their heads. When you break down the demographics, it is roughly the same across the board—whether men are old or young, happily married or single, religious or not.

The Tom Cruise Conversation

One day, shortly after the release of *Mission: Impossible II,* Jeff and I were riding in the car and talking over what I was discovering on this "visual" subject. Jeff confessed that he didn't understand why I was so surprised. Here's how our conversation went from there:

> *Jeff:* But you knew men are visual, right?
>
> *Me:* Well, yes, of course. But since most women aren't, I just didn't get it. I just don't experience things the same way you do.
>
> *Jeff:* See, I'm not sure I really believe that.
>
> *Me:* Well, it's true!
>
> *Jeff:* Maybe we just use different language to describe it. For example, think of a movie star that you find physically attractive—Tom Cruise, say. After we've seen one of his movies, how many times will that attractive image rise up in your mind the next day?
>
> *Me:* Never.

Jeff: I must not be explaining myself correctly. I mean, how many times will a thought of what he looked like with his shirt off just sort of pop up in your head?

Me: Never.

Jeff: Never as in *never*?

Me: Zero times. It just doesn't happen.

Jeff (after a long pause): Wow.

That was the end of that conversation, but it wasn't the end of the issue. When my husband then told this story to our small church group, he confessed that at first he thought I was embarrassed to admit that I really might have pictures of Tom Cruise in my head! It wasn't until he watched me tell the story to a group of women—and watched most of them say "never" right along with me—that the lightning bolt hit.

Our little exchange did more to teach Jeff and me how each of us is wired—and *not* wired—than almost anything else. And I hope my new understanding is helping me be more supportive and protective of my husband in today's culture.

Men in a Minefield

For those of us who aren't visual, it's hard to imagine that a man could have no control over those images popping up in his head. But as it turns out, there is a sort of shortcut for certain memories that bypasses the thinking centers of the brain.

Experts trace it to the amygdala, a part of the brain that acts as a kind of repository for memories that are tied to gut-level responses—such as a man's instinctive reaction to a provocatively dressed woman. Visceral memories from that kind of stimulation can bypass the thinking centers to involuntarily pop back up in a person's mind. While a woman's brain (more oriented toward processing emotion) is more likely to have emotional pop-up memories, men's pop-ups are more likely to be visual images.

Now, knowing about that brain wiring, imagine what today's sex-saturated culture must be like for a man. It is an environment filled with overt images that, biblically speaking, they were never supposed to have to face. The very act of living today for a man becomes an unasked-for walk through a minefield of possible triggers and unwanted images that can pop up again days or years later.

Consider this common example: A prime-time television commercial flashes a sensual two-second image—say, of a woman undressing—that is up on the screen and gone before the man can look away. *Boom,* nothing he can do. And it can end up in his mental photo files even if he doesn't want it there.

Mental Photo Files on Autoactivate

When I asked men how often a sensual thought or image barged into their consciousness, many of them said something like, "All the time." Of course, I wanted to know what "All the time" meant!

"If you're talking about a teenage boy, 'all the time' means *all the time*," one forty-year-old man explained. "It would be fairly unusual for a teenage guy to go a couple of hours without an involuntary image—and then when he does, he could spend half an hour straight on the subject. A twenty-something man also has a pretty difficult time. Once you reach your thirties and forties, you're a little more settled and those thoughts are more often triggered by something."

And once those thoughts are triggered, he and others clarified, the man has to make a great effort to tear them down (if, that is, he is the type of man who wants to keep his thought life pure). They also said that the longer a man entertains the temptation, the more difficult it will be to get rid of.

THIS IS NORMAL?

Okay, let's take a deep breath for a second. For some of us, this is a lot to take in. For others, it's no big deal. Also, if you are visual, you may more readily understand the struggle experienced by a husband, boyfriend, or son. And don't worry—you're normal. But it's important for the rest of us to realize that our men are normal too. As the national survey showed, this temptation is

common to nearly every man. And as my interviewees emphasized, it has no bearing on their devotion to their wives.

Before we go any further, we should make a critical distinction: temptations are not sins. The Bible states that Jesus was
"tempted in every way, just as we are—yet was without sin."
What we do with those temptations is the issue, and we'll get to
that in a moment.

For now, remembering the brain wiring involved, let's sort
out the progression of male responses to see which are involuntary and which most definitely are not.

> Temptations are not sins. What we do with
> those temptations is the issue.

Step 1: For Every Man, Sensual Images and Thoughts Arrive Involuntarily

Daniel Weiss, media and sexuality analyst at Focus on the Family, told me, "I would emphasize to women that, yes, men do have
these thoughts whether they want them or not."

In addition, if the stimulus is there (a great figure in a tight
outfit), so is the response. As one man put it, "It doesn't even
register that I thought *great body* until two seconds later!" Most
men, it appears, cannot prevent that initial response.

Don't believe me? Let me illustrate.

Don't read this.

No really, don't read it. Just look at the letters.

Impossible, isn't it? There is no way to just notice the letters without reading the word. That's what it's like for a guy. His brain is wired to read "good body" without his even realizing it.

Step 2: Every Man's Involuntary Physical Impulse Is to Enjoy the Feelings Associated with These Thoughts and Images

Because men are hard-wired to be sexual hunters, every thought and image related to that pursuit comes associated with powerful feelings. When a sensual image enters a man's mind (or a great body enters his line of sight), it brings a rush of sexual pleasure— a short-term pleasure that, we must remember, was supposed to be tied to the only such images he would ever see…those of his wife! But in today's world of unavoidable tight-miniskirt and spaghetti-strap visuals, hopefully the man denies himself that short-term rush in order to honor God, his wife, or his mental purity and thus establish deeper pleasure down the road.

> Hopefully, the man denies himself the short-term pleasure in order to honor his wife.

But again, the initial physical sensation of enjoyment is involuntary. A few years after the original edition of this book came out, Jeff and I were at a crowded mall with our then six-year-old daughter and four-year-old son, and at one point we realized that our little boy was no longer at our side. Panicked, we ran back through the mall looking for him—only to find him standing stock-still in front of the Victoria's Secret window. There he was, staring thunderstruck at the life-size photographs of the models wearing...not much. Just as I thought to myself, *Oh shoot,* he raised his little arm and pointed. His voice held a note of awe.

"I like those ladies."

I nudged my husband, who bent down and said, "Yes, um, they are very pretty. What do you like about those ladies?"

"Their bare tummies," he said, and gestured to his own stomach. "Makes my tummy feel good." He was four years old and had no idea what sex was, but he still had a male brain.

One married man described the physical sensations associated with enticing thoughts and images this way: "When an image plays on a man's brain or he gazes at an attractive woman, it's not just pure lust. There's a thrill there. And a man can go back to that adrenaline rush by entertaining those images."

In my clinical research for *The Lights of Tenth Street,* I heard over and over again how enticing that visual sensation is for men and how difficult it is to resist. This factual insight into a man's inner life may help us understand why some men can make a series of wrong choices and end up struggling in some way with pornography.

Step 3: But Every Man Can Make a Choice— to Dwell on the Images and Thoughts or to Dismiss Them

This choice is the critical distinction between temptation and sin. Once an image intrudes in a man's head, either he can linger on it and possibly even start a mental parade into serious lust, or he can tear it down immediately and "take every thought captive," as the Bible puts it.

> Men I talked to make rigorous decisions to avoid unwanted visual invitations.

Most of the men I talked to take this choice extremely seriously. They make rigorous decisions to avoid unwanted visual invitations, to turn away from those that arise, and—when unwanted pictures arise anyway—to rip them down with all sorts of diversionary tactics. I hear that mentally running through baseball scores, household projects, and stored images of their wives were popular thought substitutes for many men. Honestly, it sounds exhausting.

So, although few men can stop an involuntary image from popping up in their heads, and few men can stop themselves from wanting to look, they can (and often do) exercise the discipline to stop themselves from actually doing so. On the survey, the biggest factor in whether a man made this choice wasn't whether he was older, married, or happy in his relationship (all of those mattered, but in small numbers). It was whether he regularly attended religious services. Confirming this, nearly half of the men on the follow-up churchgoers' survey said they would try to stop themselves from looking.

It is vital that we understand just how much strength and discipline that choice requires so that we can appreciate what our men try to do for us every day in this minefield of a culture.

AND NOW FOR SOME REASSURANCES...

After all these generalizations, it's vital to recognize the critical reassuring elements that are just as much a part of your man's inner life.

Reassurance 1: He Probably Wishes He Could Reserve His Visual Nature Just for You

Most men I spoke with said they enjoy being visual but wish they could reserve it entirely for their wives. They disliked having to face the temptations that abound today, the distractions at work, and the struggle to keep their thought lives pure. Many men echoed this husband's sentiment: "You have to realize: If men could, most would shut off their temptation to look at other women in a second. We loathe this temptation as much as our wives do!"

"Most men would shut off this temptation in a second if we could. We loathe this temptation as much as our wives do!"

Reassurance 2: He Can See a Beautiful Woman Without the Sexual Temptation

One distinction I heard repeatedly from men was that his "wanting to look" temptation often wasn't sexual at all. Instinctive? Yes. Physical? Sure. But not necessarily sexual.

One man told me, "What you may not realize is that a lot of this is simply about admiring beauty. It's like looking at a painting. You're not just thinking, *Let's go to a motel and shack up.* Women don't necessarily look at a man and admire him as a thing of beauty, but men will do that. It's like walking through an art gallery. A man might look, despite himself. But it's not necessarily a sexual thing."

Reassurance 3: Every Man Is Different—and Discipline Makes a Difference

Also, because every man is different, every man experiences a different level of visual temptation. For some men, an involuntary sensual image may be little more than a nuisance, while others might find it a real stumbling block.

Here's a comparison that some of us might recognize all too well. At a dessert party, I might struggle for two hours with the fact that a chocolate mousse cake is across the room, calling my name. But the person standing next to me might be able to put that temptation out of her mind. (Don't you just hate those people!) Similarly, the ongoing practice of self-discipline in turning away from the chocolate cake—or the provocative scene on the television screen—is likely to make that type of self-discipline easier next time. Many men I talked to have invested many years into taking "every thought captive" in this culture.

Reassurance 4: It's Not Because of You

Upon learning all of this, some of us may secretly wonder, *What's wrong with me? Am I not attractive enough?* I have gotten enough anguished e-mails to know that many women suspect that their husbands' struggles arise because of their flaws, not just because they are men. But hearing these truths from every man I interviewed made clear to me that this truly is—as the title of a popular book puts it—*Every Man's Battle.*[11]

In the biblical book of Job, the title character makes a telling statement: "I made a covenant with my eyes not to look with lust upon a young woman." Why would Job need to take such a step? After all, God describes him as "the finest man in all the earth" and "a man of complete integrity." Surely, the finest man in all the earth wouldn't even have this struggle!

But you see, Job had a male brain.

You love your husband as a man, and this is part of what makes him a man. Even if you were a bikini model, your husband would still have this vulnerability.

Reassurance 5: This Doesn't Impact His Feelings for You!

Finally, and most important, we must grasp this fact: a man's biological temptation has, as one man put it, "no impact whatsoever on my feelings for my wife." A man married more than twenty-five years explained,

> There is no relationship with the woman who catches your eye. With your wife, you have a deep and long and meaningful relationship. There is no competition there. Yes, your mind may make the observation that this other woman is twenty years younger and has never had two kids. But that is all it is—an observation. And that observation is immediately offset by other factors, such as the fact that you love your wife!

In one small-group interview, all the men agreed with that statement and added, in the words of one, "It is truly just an observation. There is nothing on earth that would be worth the price of going beyond that. I would *never* risk losing my wife."

SO WHAT'S A WOMAN TO DO?

For many of us, on these issues it would be so easy to move from understanding, to alarm, to the Charge of the Light Brigade—to get anxious or suspicious of our men and get all fired up to change them. But in the book's introduction, I said that these revelations are meant to change *us*. Of course, men can and should do things to keep their thought lives pure. Men should do whatever is necessary to honor the women they love. But many such books have been written and programs created for men by expert psychiatrists, counselors, and ministry leaders, including our challenge to the men in *For Men Only*. But this book is for us women, alone.

So what do we do?

Pray For Him—and For Yourself

Prayer is the most powerful and meaningful way to partner with the men in our lives, but it's often the most overlooked. There's a little verse in Psalm 127: "Unless the LORD protects a city, guarding it with sentries will do no good." We can work to help and protect our husbands and our marriages, but in the end, that's the Lord's job. So it is vital to cover your husband, boyfriend, or son in prayer from the onslaughts of this culture.

Similarly, if you are feeling despair at these revelations, or a desire to hound and punish your man for his wiring, that is *not* from the Lord. Just as men have to "take every thought captive," so do we have to take captive those worries that threaten to spiral out of control (which could deeply hurt our marriages). If you find yourself with any kind of insecurity about this, ask God to protect your heart as well.

Check Your Heart

Before we can truly support our men, we must first take stock of our willingness to support our men in the way they need to be supported. Consider this plea, from the follow-up churchgoers' survey:

> To accept the struggle I have with lust, and encourage me rather than freak out and conclude the worst about me. The more I can reveal my weaknesses without being judged or accused, or without a major crisis in our relationship resulting from my transparency, the more I know I am loved for who I am, not for who she wants me to be.

Do we love the men in our lives for who they are or for who we want them to be? Do we want to support our husbands or to change them?

The way you answer those questions makes a world of difference. And of course, the only person you can actually change is yourself. If you aren't sure you can address the issue with the right heart, you might want to spend some time praying and asking God for *His,* before you do anything.

Do we love the men in our lives for who they are or for who we want them to be?

That is especially important given the fact that men vary widely in how much they wrestle with this, and how ready they are to deal with it. When there is a real issue, I have seen how important it is for a wife to be able to handle it with maturity and care—even when she doesn't feel like it! And when there isn't a true problem, I've also seen how destructive it is for a wife to become hurt or suspicious when it is not warranted.

Become a Support

If you and your husband would like to work together, here are some ideas to get you started.

- *Let your husband know that you are willing to talk about this and that you understand the difficulties he must face every day.* Ask what you can do to help. Put yourself on his team to help him win this fight. Daniel Weiss gave me great insight on this:

The best thing women can do to help their husbands is to practice two of the most crucial elements of a marriage—openness and honesty. Things that drive anyone dealing with sexual sin are shame, guilt, and secrecy. If the guy has secrecy, if there isn't a safe place to talk about what is a real temptation for guys, then chances are it's going to get worse. The best thing women can do is to let men know that it is all right for them to share their temptation if they want to.

- *Notice and appreciate your husband's efforts to honor you.* Keep your antenna up, and you'll be surprised by just how many daily choices he must make to keep his thought life pure in this culture.

Now that my radar is on, not only does my husband not resent my new awareness; he actually appreciates it. Because now I see the girl in the tight outfit—and I notice when Jeff is tense with the effort of not looking. And instead of being upset that he was attracted, I love him for the effort he is making to honor me.

- *Remember that, for a man, there's a fine line between your affirmation and humiliation.* No husband wants to be treated like your son ("What a good boy!"). But you *can* notice if your husband turns away from the latest provocative commercial, give him a quick grin, and say, "Thank you." Many women, when out with their men, will even say things like, "What a beautiful girl," relieving the stress of his effort to not look. (Of course, that only works if the attractive woman evokes admiration, not lust.)

- *Recognize the common factors that make it harder for a man to stay pure.* Several organizations mention the HALT checklist: Hungry, Angry, Lonely, Tired. When a man is working long hours, is out of sorts with the world (or you), feels unappreciated, feels like a failure, or is far from home on a business trip, he's likely to become more vulnerable. If you've ever found yourself eating the entire box of cookies when you feel unhappy, you understand this dynamic.

- *Know your limits.* Some men will have gone beyond normal struggles and into dangerous or addictive behaviors and need your encouragement as they seek specialized help (see forwomenonlybook.com for some starting points). Further, counselors in this area agree that while there needs to be an open husband-wife dialogue no matter what, if a true struggle has arisen, the husband's primary account-ability partner must be male. One said, "It would be destructive if the wife becomes the police. Men don't need a critique but an encourager."

The key is to understand what is helpful in *your* marriage. Every man and every marriage is different. Ask him what makes him feel appreciated or makes his struggle easier, and then do it.

Champion Modesty in Yourself and Others

Let's face it, women and girls who are totally clueless about this problem can also thoughtlessly contribute to it. After all, the images in a man's mental photo files come from somewhere—and it's not just from pictures. The eye magnets on the street are choosing to dress the way they do.

> Women and girls who are clueless about this problem can thoughtlessly contribute to it.

Unfortunately, because many women don't have the same type of visual brain wiring, we may not understand what we are doing to the men around us—a fact that men find hard to believe, by the way. One father asked me why his normally cautious college-aged daughter dressed in a tight little top and skirt around a particular guy she found attractive. "Surely," this father said, "surely she knows what she's doing!"

"Yes," I agreed, "she knows she looks good. But she doesn't

realize what is actually going on in that guy's head. What she's smugly thinking is, *He thinks I'm cute.*"

"Cute has nothing to do with it!" the shocked father replied. "He's picturing her *naked*!"

And that is what we often don't get. Many women and teen girls are just longing for male love and attention, not realizing that the resulting attention is the wrong kind and has nothing to do with love.

After I researched *For Young Women Only,* one youth leader presented my findings on teen boys' visual wiring at a youth retreat. She e-mailed me to say that the girls talked to the boys about it during the entire bus ride home. When they arrived, they were so convicted about how they had unwittingly been causing the guys to stumble that they got off the bus, threw all their Soffe shorts into a Dumpster, and marched straight over to the mall to find outfits that were cute without being sexually tempting.

Unfortunately, I can also guarantee that many adult women reading this book are unwitting fodder for the mental photo files of some devoted married man just because of how they dress. It's natural to enjoy being noticed, but he doesn't want you in there. You're cluttering up a good husband's mind and tempting him to dishonor his wife.

It is our responsibility to ensure that, as much as it depends on us, this doesn't happen.

PUT IT IN PERSPECTIVE

Remember that, in God's plan, the only woman a man was ever supposed to see in an intimate way was his wife—and those pop-up visuals would make sure that, regardless of how far afield a man had to roam to feed his family (whether that meant ancient hunting trips or modern airplane trips), he'd have special images of his wife to keep him company and spur him to get back home.

It used to be that a man had to seek out visual temptations. Today they are impossible to avoid. So spend your energy helping him fight temptations instead of fighting him.

God doesn't make mistakes. One of my closest friends relates that, as a new bride of twenty-three, she was shaken to discover that her husband had this issue with his thought life. She cried out to God, "Why did You create him like this?" And then she realized: God *did* create him like this, and He said His creation was good.

> God created men like this. And He said His creation was good.

We are all fallible, but we are also created the way we are for a purpose. Whether or not other things have gotten in the way, that good purpose is still there—for you and for the man you love.

Eight

CHOCOLATE, FLOWERS, BAIT FISHING

Why the Reluctant Romeo You Know Really Does Want Romance

Men enjoy romance (sometimes in different ways than women) and want to be romantic— but hesitate because they doubt they can succeed.

Our culture often depicts men as a bunch of clods who have no desire to be romantic. The husband who buys his wife a belt sander for Valentine's Day is the hilarious backbone of many a television sitcom or movie. One amusing example comes from the classic movie *When Harry Met Sally*. Harry (played by Billy Crystal) explains to Sally (Meg Ryan) what goes through his head immediately after a sexual encounter:

Harry: How long do I have to lie here and hold her....

Is thirty seconds enough?

Sally (shocked): That's what you're thinking?[12]

Are men really clods when it comes to romance—or do they just think about it differently than we do? Do they really write it off as a big waste of time? Or is it just something they're happy to put up with as long as they get sex afterward?

> Are men really clods when it comes to romance—or do they just think about it differently than we do?

You might be in for a big surprise. According to my findings, most men feel that they *are* secret romantics who—like most of us—don't experience nearly as much intimacy in their primary love relationship as they'd like. Even more surprising, this desire is (in a way) quite apart from sexual intimacy. The great news is that our men long for connection, togetherness, and fun, intimate time...with us!

MEN WANT ROMANCE TOO

I have to confess, I truly was shocked to discover this. On my very first informal test survey of ten men, when I asked if they desired romance *for themselves,* every single respondent chose "Yes, very much"—and I realized that I had inadvertently bought into the popular notion that men really don't care.

As you can see from the survey, the vast majority of men actively enjoy and desire romance.

Regardless of whether you are able to plan romantic events, or whether your wife/significant other appreciates it, do you, yourself, desire romance? (Choose one answer.)

Yes, very much or yes, somewhat.		84%
I can take it or leave it.		14%
I don't care for it.		2%

0%   50%   100%

Their answers held regardless of whether the men were old or young, married or unmarried. As one survey taker put it, "I wish my wife knew that I need romance, that I need touching and hugs as much as she does." Listen to what one man told me about one of those romantically awkward moments we all recognize:

On our honeymoon, we were in the Caribbean and were at this dinner place with a dance floor, and no one was dancing. So of course my wife says, "Let's go dance." I'm risking humiliation, but I go. And within ninety seconds, the dance floor was full. Someone had to risk it. Most of the women in the restaurant probably thought that the other couples didn't think about dancing until we gave them the idea. But I guarantee every guy in that place *was* thinking about it and didn't want to risk it until someone else did.

Men want romance, just as we do. In the pages ahead, we'll talk about how to get past the awkwardness and misunderstanding and move in that direction. And we'll listen to the men (every last Cary Grant one of them) tell us how to do it.

WHY MEN DON'T MAKE A MOVE

When I've told women that they're probably married to a closet romantic, I usually hear the puzzled refrain, "Well, if they want to do romantic things, why don't they?"

> "If they want to do romantic things, why don't they?"

The male responses fall into two catchall categories: internal hesitation and the gender gap in definitions of romance. Consider the enlightening survey results:

Suppose you had to plan an anniversary event for your wife/significant other. Do you know how to put together a romantic event that you know your partner would enjoy? (Choose one answer.)

Yes, I can do it with style.		54%
Yes, but I'm not sure that I would do a very good job.		34%
No, she may not like what I did.		8%
No, I really don't have a clue.		4%

Notice that a huge majority (88 percent) felt they could probably put together a romantic event. So in addition to caring more about romance than we might have thought, these men also had a better idea (than, say, your average clod) of what romance might look like. But the survey also shows the problem: almost half (46 percent) feel unsure of themselves and aren't confident you'll like their romantic efforts.

> Almost half of men aren't confident you'll like their romantic efforts.

As I spoke with the men, I heard three distinct concerns that caused them to hesitate.

Internal Hesitation 1: "I Won't Do a Very Good Job"

Apparently, many of us have overlooked the most basic stumbling block to our men's romantic initiative: self-doubt. Many men just feel clumsy in romance. As one guy said, "We do feel like clods sometimes. It's like trying to write with your left hand."

A single man brought up the impostor issue: "I try to just do it without being found out," he said. "No guy really knows how—they just play the game like what they've seen."

When you factor in how performance oriented men are (how much they want to *do* things, do them well, and be affirmed for it), this self-doubt can translate into hesitation—or doing nothing at all—even if inside the man is yearning for romance.

One man described the tension: "The flip side of the need for respect is horror at the idea of humiliation. I'd rather burn at the stake. That's why a man won't risk trying to be romantic. I'm risking humiliation if I do it wrong."

Another man explained his anxiety this way: "The reason men practice sports so much is so they don't get embarrassed on the field—so they don't feel inadequate. But there's no way to practice romance. So if they don't know how, they figure it's best not to even approach it and risk being seen as inadequate."

Believe it or not, a man's willingness to take romantic risks may also be tied to how he's feeling about his job. A man who feels stressed and inadequate at work may feel particularly unable to risk feeling inadequate at home—in which case, it would feel safer for him to do nothing.

Internal Hesitation 2: Haunted by Romantic Failures

As you can now guess, if our men seem thoughtless or unromantic, they may simply be taking a safe course after what was (in their minds) a painful romantic failure in the past.

Because men often feel like romantic klutzes, they are incredibly sensitive to criticism or teasing. One man said flatly, "You tease me about not quite getting the candlelight dinner right, that's it—it'll be five years before I try it again."

"You tease me about not quite getting the candlelight dinner right, it'll be five years before I try it again."

Another man relayed this story. "I spent a ton of time finding this special present for her birthday, and I was really jazzed about it. When she opened it, she smiled and said, 'Thanks, sweetheart,' kissed me on the cheek, and started talking about going out to dinner. I felt like, after all that time and effort, I didn't quite get it right. Next time I think it will be better just to aim low and be safe."

Some men have the opposite problem—scoring a romantic success only to be paralyzed by the idea of having to top it. With my husband's blessing, I share an example.

For years I was puzzled by a feast-or-famine trend where Jeff would sometimes go all out to craft a romantic gift but would other times sheepishly give me a gift card. When we lived in Manhattan, he surprised me one Valentine's Day with a children's book about a little girl who longed for ice-skating lessons—just as I always had.

On the page where the girl finally got her dream, he had taped a brochure for a month of private ice-skating lessons with Olympian JoJo Starbuck at Rockefeller Center. I would also meet gold medalists Katarina Witt and Scott Hamilton. I was thrilled and told everyone I knew!

But then I didn't get a romantic gift for the next three years. I was puzzled until Jeff confessed. He was sure that he would never be able to top that Valentine's Day reaction, so he just shut down. "Guys are so competitive, and I'm even competitive with myself. I was sure that the next one wouldn't be as good, so there was no way to win."

Thankfully, I was able to convince him that anything he put thought into made me feel special, which made it safe for him to try.

Internal Hesitation 3: It's Difficult to Change Gears

Even working women may not appreciate how tough it is for a man to switch from the fast-paced, highly practical attitude of work to the tenderness of romance. And my male interviewees have assured me that we shouldn't take this phenomenon personally—they just need space to relax and refresh for a while.

> The men assured me that we shouldn't take personally their need to decompress after work.

And everyone transitions differently. We've already seen how men need time to let go of so much of the workday stuff in their minds, through something like crashing on the couch or mowing the lawn. But for some men, their means of transitioning is totally different. One high-energy friend, who travels with a stressful job, told me he used to arrive home and "bulldoze the house." Then he realized he wasn't leaving his work attitudes at the door and that "it was hurting my wife's feelings," he said. "Now she recognizes that I need help to transition, so she asks me questions, and I babble for about forty-five minutes. Before I know it, I am moving into 'home mode' because I have been able to unload my work issues in a safe environment. Plus I build greater rapport with my wife at the same time."

Almost every man I talked to said he needs to decompress somehow before he can think about being a romantic, loving husband. And if his wife can understand and give him that time, he'll be happier and more available the rest of the evening.

BRIDGING THE DEFINITION GAP

One of my test surveys was of fifty men on a retreat. When I asked the question, "Do you, yourself, desire romance?" one of the men answered, "Yes, very much," but added in the margin, "But we have different definitions." That led me to want to find out what definitions of romance women may have missed.

Redefinition 1: Playing Together Is Very Romantic

Men want to go out and do things together with their wives, and they view that as incredibly romantic. Playing with their wives makes them feel close and loving and intimate; it offers an escape from the ordinary, a time to focus on each other—all things that women also want from romance.

> Men want to go out and do things together with their wives, and they view that as incredibly romantic.

Here's a great insight from one husband:

Most married men don't want to abandon their wife to do guy things. They want to do "guy things" with their wife. They want her to be their playmate. It's no different from when they were dating. For a guy, a big part of the thrill was doing fun things together.

The woman who is having fun with her husband is incredibly attractive. If you see a woman out playing golf with her husband, I guarantee that all the other guys are jealous. Getting out and having fun together falls off in marriage because of various responsibilities, but men still want to *play* with their wives.

Once I heard this—over and over, I might add—I was able to see certain things in a new light. My husband is actually relatively interested in traditional candlelight-and-flowers-type romance— but perhaps more for my sake than his.

Talking to all these men opened my eyes to all the times I didn't fully realize that some activity Jeff suggested would have been romantic for him. In his mind, the activity wasn't just a fun day of hiking or a chance to relax and walk around a quaint little town nearby—it was his version of a candlelight dinner. Recognizing that made it much more fun to jump on the opportunity and appreciate all that it meant.

Men sometimes have different notions of what is romantic. If you take sex out of the equation, which of the following do you find more romantic for yourself? (Choose one answer.)

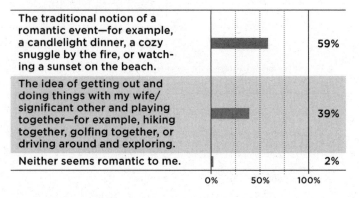

The traditional notion of a romantic event—for example, a candlelight dinner, a cozy snuggle by the fire, or watching a sunset on the beach.	59%
The idea of getting out and doing things with my wife/significant other and playing together—for example, hiking together, golfing together, or driving around and exploring.	39%
Neither seems romantic to me.	2%

0%   50%   100%

While almost 60 percent of the men on the follow-up survey desired the traditional definition of romance, almost 40 percent said they preferred a more active approach. Perhaps you, like me, have been missing opportunities to enjoy a romantic time with your mate just because you didn't realize it *was* romantic!

Redefinition 2: Romance Without Sex May Not Feel Complete

You can guess from the sex chapter that men consider sex a part of romance. It doesn't always have to be connected, and it doesn't have to happen at the same time, but trust me: when he's romancing you, sex is in the back of his mind.

To make a giant generalization, women can often experience emotional closeness and feel that an evening is romantically complete without sex, but men often can't. Consider these representative comments:

- "It is hard for men to delineate romance without sex. It's all part of it. If men are romantic, they want sex. If there were no moral or societal constraints, romance would always lead to sex."

- "I love setting up a romantic evening, but it is a lot of work for me. And I don't think my wife realizes that, when I am being romantic, I've got a very specific end point in mind. So sometimes there's intense disappointment after all that work!"

- "The guy is thinking, *If romance is about feeling emotionally connected, and sex is my way of being emotionally connected, and we're* already *being romantic, then why not now? If we're going to have sex sometime in the next month, wouldn't now be a good time?*"

Another man brought up the unfortunate dynamic where a husband uses romance to get sex or a wife uses sex to get romance. But he provided an alternative view:

If a wife only "gives" sex to get something she wants, that is so hurtful to a guy. Sex should not be made a payout after a guy works to earn his wife's favor. A guy wants romance not to somehow manipulate sex but to reexperience the spark of dating, to reconnect after days of draining work at the office, to feel love and intimacy, to know he is wanted and enjoyed, and to utterly escape the crushing nonstop pressure of life. And sex can be a wonderful part of all that. Romance is all about escaping—escaping with the person you love and discovering to one's monumental delight that she, too, wants to escape—with me!

Clearly, just as we want our husbands to love us in the way we need to be loved, our men want the same. And sex is a huge part of making them feel loved.

THE POWER OF A WOMAN IN LOVE

Is it dawning on you just how much power we women have to change the whole romance picture? More than likely, we each live with a motivated man who wants more romantic closeness but who is holding back or frustrated. Which means we often hold the key to the quality of romance.

If you've been disappointed with your romantic relationship and have pushed and prodded to no effect, you've probably realized that nagging doesn't work. So how do we start?

Encourage Him

Although a man always needs his wife's appreciation, it is especially critical when he is outside his comfort zone—which, when it comes to romance, is probably the case for half the male population.

One man was blunt: "Encourage me and affirm my efforts, and I'll run through a brick wall to please you. But don't just assume that I know you're pleased. I'm way outside my comfort zone. I'm willing to be a fool for you, but just tell me that I did good. And give me sex. That helps too."

Remember that many men view taking romantic initiative as a huge risk—a risk of being humiliated or feeling inadequate. So prove to your man that it's not a risk! When he makes an effort, it's your responsibility—and your joy—to demonstrate that it was worth it.

Even when your man isn't outside his comfort zone, he can become frustrated when you don't want to "go outside and play" when the opportunity arises. So next time he suggests something, don't tell him you really need to vacuum the house. Give him his version of a candlelight dinner, and enjoy your romantic time together!

Entice Him

Just as men want to be encouraged, they want to be enticed. One married man relayed this interchange with a female friend who was wondering why romance sometimes dies off in marriage.

> *Her:* Romance is the sense that you're still being pursued.
> *Him:* But we caught you. Hand me the remote.

Many men have told me that, whether in work or in romance, they are always looking for something to conquer—something to "catch." A key element in keeping romance alive is to keep giving that to our husbands.

Keep it fresh—give him something new to pursue. Go hiking with him. Play golf with him. Give him space when he needs it, and intimate attention when he needs that. Make yourself the kind of friend and lover he constantly wants to pursue.

Make yourself the kind of friend and lover that your man constantly wants to pursue.

Tell Harry What Sally Needs

Several men suggested that, since they can't read our minds, it's fine for us to drop hints about those romantic things we'd like to do…as long as they truly are hints, not directives. Take that classic Harry-and-Sally issue: cuddling. Because cuddling tends to be more important to us than to guys, a little patient reeducation may be in order. And this applies to anything you find particularly romantic that he doesn't get. "Help me understand why it's so important to you," one man suggested. "Help me see that, as I romance you in *your* way, you'll be more motivated to romance me in *my* way."

This approach isn't a damaging, withholding-based model. It is learning to give what the other person needs and enjoying the resulting God-ordained fruits of that selflessness. One man's response to the cuddling example was, "Men can learn to enjoy a time of closeness after sex. And in this case, it is definitely in our best interest to understand why it matters so much to you!"

Keep Him Number One

If we let too many other priorities interfere with romance, it puts a damper on the man's enthusiasm. One of the most common concerns I heard is that we may unconsciously prioritize our kids over our husbands. On the survey, several men expressed concern that "she spends too much time doting on the children" and not enough time doting on the relationship.

A man with three active children commented, "It's considered a Christian thing to do, to be with the kids all the time. But for me as a man, there is a sense of 'I've lost my wife.' It could sound selfish, but it's not. And it's not too healthy for the kids either."

One man said, "It's not just kids that steal a wife. It's the whole to-do list. Even helping others can get in the way."

> We have a tremendous opportunity to start over with our men.

That is the cry of a man who just wants to spend more quality, romantic time with his wife. What an irony, considering that most women pine for the same thing! We have a tremendous opportunity to start over with our men...and in the process rediscover the delight of the mutual pursuit.

Nine

THE TRUTH ABOUT TAKING CARE OF YOURSELF

Why What's on the Outside Matters to Him on the Inside

You don't need to be a size 3, but your man does need to see you making the effort to take care of yourself—and he'll willingly help you.

Warning! Before you read any further, pray first! I'm not kidding. We're going to navigate some tricky waters here, and to get the most out of this, you'll need to be open to something you may not have heard before, while being protected from hurt. So take a moment now, and ask the Lord to shepherd your process of reading and absorbing this material.

• • •

Okay, ready? This chapter is about something our men desperately want us to know but feel absolutely unable to tell us: The effort you put into your appearance is extremely high on his priority list. Yet the chances that you know his true feelings are extremely low.

What I've learned about men's needs in this area—including my husband's—has been life changing. It has jarred me out of a dangerous complacency. Perhaps it will jar you out of yours.

OUT, BLIND SPOT

Call me naive, but I just didn't realize that a wife's or girlfriend's appearance was such a big deal—such an *imperative* deal—for the guy. Important, yes. Imperative, no. Of course, having learned just how visual men are, I should have gotten a clue. But somehow I assumed that if I was out of shape, I was the only person who was negatively affected.

Then one day, after speaking to a mixed group about the other topics in this book, I was approached by a man I've known professionally for several years. I'll call him Ted. He asked if we could talk privately, and we found some chairs away from everyone else.

"There's something I need to mention to you," Ted said, looking uncomfortable. "I think women have a blind spot in an area that they really need to understand." Taking a deep breath, he spilled the beans. "I don't think women know how important it is to take care of themselves and not to look like slouches around their husbands."

"You mean, not to be overweight…?" I ventured.

"That's part of it, but that's not really *it*," Ted continued. "It doesn't mean you have to be a size 3. The bigger issue is that your husband sees that you are putting forth the effort to take care of yourself…for him. See, my wife is 115 pounds, but her weight isn't really the issue. It's not about being tiny. If she doesn't take care of herself, dresses sloppily around me all the time, never exercises, and has no energy to go out and do things together, I feel like she's choosing not to do something that she should know is important to me. And then it becomes a real issue because it affects her ability to do things and her self-worth and desire—and then it affects me."

> "I just want to see that my wife cares enough about me to make an effort."

That burden off his chest, Ted relaxed. "You may not believe this," he said with a chuckle, "but it's not about whether we want our wives to prance around the house in a Little Bo Peep outfit—although that would be great too. I mean, who are we kidding! But really, I just want to see that my wife cares enough about me to make an effort."

Ever since I decided to add a chapter about this issue, the male response has been astonishing. In fact, when I describe all the topics of the book to a guy, do you know which one he is most likely to seize on as something he wished his wife understood? You got it—*this one* (sex and respect were close seconds). Most of the men who hear about this subject thank me: "Thank you for saying what we are thinking but could never, ever say." "Thank you for taking on a subject that is so taboo, especially in Christian circles."

A FEW THINGS
I'M NOT SAYING

Now, nearly all women have some form of body insecurity that we already worry about too much, and I'm not trying to add fuel to that fire! We're hammered relentlessly by media messages that we should all be perfectly shaped and eternally young. But God didn't create us to be Barbie dolls, and those fake and impossible ideals only drive women into eating disorders and other miserable, unhealthy obsessions. This chapter is *only* dealing with weight, fitness, and appearance issues that we can healthfully do something about.

So first, let's celebrate our God-given individuality—sturdy thighs, small boobs, and all—and make the best of them. Men don't mind less-than-ideal proportions. In fact, most men I spoke with wished their partners weren't so sensitive about their bodies.

Second, if you're one of those rare women who is a size 2 and convinced you're fat, be careful. You're probably delusional. This chapter is not trying to get you to lose weight. If what you read here puts you in a panic, please talk to a trusted friend or a medical advisor.

Third, we need to accept how complicated and hypersensitive the appearance issue is for both partners. Many men, for example, feel that they shouldn't care about appearance, but they do. Many women, on the other hand, feel that true love should come with no strings attached. Still, we want to be attractive. And while we were delighted that he liked our looks during courtship, we can find ourselves feeling outright resentful that our appearance still matters so much to him now. (Do you see what I mean when I say *complicated*?)

Finally, please understand that this entire subject isn't ultimately about being tiny or any other current ideal of attractiveness. Primarily, it is about showing our men that we're willing to make the effort to address something that is very important to them.

> This subject isn't about being tiny. It is about showing our men that we're willing to make the effort on something important to them.

So, with grace and good intentions firmly in hand, let's take a hard look at what men really think.

EVERY MAN CARES

Almost every man cares if his wife is out of shape and doesn't make a true effort to change. For some it's merely a wistful "Oh, for the good old days" sigh, while for others it's a relationship wrecker. Here's what I asked on the survey:

Imagine your wife/significant other is overweight, wears baggy sweats when you are home, and only does her hair and makeup to go out. She hates being overweight, but nothing much changes and lately you've seen her eating more sweets. What goes through your mind? (Choose all correct answers.)

It doesn't bother me at all.	12%
It emotionally bothers me (aggregated from those who chose one or more answers such as "I know it shouldn't bother me, but it does.").	70%
I want her to make an effort to take care of herself—not just for herself, but also for me.	47%
This question doesn't apply to me because my wife/significant other already looks great all the time, and I can't imagine her otherwise.	20%

0%   50%   100%

Note: because men could choose more than one answer, percentages do not add up to total 100 percent.

Seven out of ten men indicated that they would be emotionally bothered if the woman in their lives let herself go *and didn't seem to want to make the effort to do something about it.* Only 12 percent said it didn't bother them—and even fewer happily married, younger, churchgoing men weren't bothered.

Once I understood this—and started making the effort myself—my husband felt safe to confirm that most guys do indeed struggle with this issue. With some trepidation, he gently reminded me of when, after our son was born, I used to eat a chocolate doughnut every morning. He said, "I know it's awful, but every morning when I saw those doughnuts on the counter, my heart would just sink. I'd think, *It's never going to change.* We guys keep our spirits up with the thought that some hope is out there—that things will change. For me, those chocolate doughnuts weren't the issue; it was that they said something about you making a choice not to get back in shape, for me."

Your Effort Is What Matters

Most of us can get paralyzed into inaction by the thought of having to look like the impossibly thin twenty-year-olds on television. But over and over again, I heard each man say that what mattered most to him was not that his wife shrank down to her honeymoon bikini but that she was willing to make the effort to take care of herself for him.

> What mattered most to him was not that his wife shrunk down to her honeymoon bikini but that she made an effort for him.

So I gathered my courage and asked the question directly:

Is this statement true or false? "I want my wife/significant other to look good and feel energetic. It is not as important that she look just like she did the day we met. It is more important that she make the effort to take care of herself for me now." (Choose one answer.)

True	83%
False	17%

0%　　　50%　　　100%

Look at the encouraging response: Five out of six men agreed—with regular churchgoers agreeing even more strongly. It's not that results don't matter; of course they do. But they will be a by-product of our efforts to take care of ourselves.

"For Better or For Worse"

Before we look further, those of us who don't believe in divorce may need to own up to creeping complacency. Think how off-limits it is in a church setting to emphasize the importance of a woman's physical appeal. "God looks not on the outward appearance but on the heart," we say, and expect our husbands to do the same. Our husbands have pledged their faithfulness for better or for worse, and we know "it's what's inside that counts."

Trouble is, we can easily migrate to the idea that what's outside doesn't matter.

But it *does*. And when we seem to be willfully ignoring that truth, our men—even godly men who are devoted to us—end up feeling disregarded, disrespected, and hurt. So let's try to understand why his feelings about your appearance can run so high, even if they're out of sight to you.

WHY DOES YOUR EFFORT IN APPEARANCE MATTER?

One man reading a draft of this chapter looked at this subject heading and exclaimed, "What do you mean, '*Why* does it matter?'!" Men really don't understand why a woman would have to ask the question. So why is it so essential? Here's what men said— when they felt safe enough to tell the truth.

"When You Take Care of Yourself, I Feel Like You Care About Me"

Since men are so visual, seeing us make the effort to look good makes them feel loved and cared for. It matters to them in the same way it matters to us when we notice our husbands making an effort to do things that make us feel loved—especially when they are things that are difficult or don't come naturally.

Consider one husband's honest comment: "My wife is trying to slim down right now, and it makes me feel like a million bucks. I know she's also doing it for herself, but the fact that she cares about how she looks is a total turnon, if you want to know the truth. I tell her all the time how much I appreciate the work she's putting into this."

If you have a hard time believing that your man really cares about your efforts as much as your results, here's a helpful romance-related parallel: If your husband truly puts effort and thought into a romantic event, do you really mind if it's not perfect? If it's your birthday and you come home from work to find that he has gotten friends to watch the kids, the house has been cleaned, and he has slaved over a meal, are you really going to care if the veal piccata is overdone? Of course not. You'll feel loved and cared for.

"When You Don't Take Care of Yourself, I Feel Unvalued and Unhappy"

How does a man feel when the woman he is married to looks significantly different than the one he courted? After I tackled this subject in one of my newspaper columns, a twenty-seven-year-old man wrote to tell me he knew many men whose wives had gained a lot of weight since their wedding days:

Shaunti, those women need to realize that their doubling in size is like a man going from being a corporate executive to a minimum-wage slacker—and assuming it has no effect on his spouse. A woman's appearance is a simple yet important part of happiness in a marriage. A number of my friends love their spouses, but are not happy, mainly for that reason.

And being out of shape affects more than just appearance. Remember how much a man wants to go out and do things with his wife—and how close that makes him feel to you? One survey taker wrote, "She is a very pretty woman, but she is not taking care of herself, so she feels bad about her looks, she has little energy, and we are limiting our opportunities, such as going to a pool party or the lake or beach."

In a way, this issue for men is like the romance issue for us. Maybe it shouldn't matter whether our husbands ever put one jot of effort into romancing us. But it does. We love them regardless, but it doesn't remove the empty wistfulness we feel or the pain we may suffer wondering why on earth our men don't see that this is so important to us.

In a way, this issue for men is like the romance issue for us.

Guys feel the same way on the issue of how we take care of ourselves. It is critical that we acknowledge that their desire is both real and legitimate.

"When You Take Care of Yourself, Your Expectation That 'I Only Have Eyes for You' Feels Fairer (and Easier to Accomplish)"

As we struggle with this hard truth, it might be helpful to remember that we're not alone. We're also asking our men to do something that is hard and goes against their natural instinct. The man who originally opened my eyes to this issue explained it this way:

> We need to see that you care about keeping our attention on you—and off of other women. Sometimes it is so hard for us to look away. It takes a lot of work and a lot of effort. But it helps me so much if I see that my wife is willing to do her part and purposefully work toward staying in shape and looking good.

"I Want (and Need) to Be Proud of You"

Several men told me something like this: "I want to be proud of my wife. Every man has this innate competition with other men, and our wives are a part of that. Every man wants other men to think that he did well in his choice of a wife."

Now, I'm going to share something that will be difficult to hear. This two-part comment is from a close friend whose heart I trust completely. I'm including it because I've found that it is truly how men think and because I believe it helps to make a critical distinction:

Sometimes I'll meet a guy who looks just like an average guy. But then, if I meet his wife and she is huge and very out of shape and just sloppy, I feel so sorry for him. It sounds terrible, but my gut just churns for him. It's this "Oh, I'm so sorry" sort of compassion. That sounds absolutely terrible to say out loud, but it is what every man is thinking.

But then sometimes I'll meet a man whose wife is overweight—but she takes care of herself. She puts some effort into her appearance. She dresses neatly or does her makeup and hair. If she is comfortable in her own skin and is confident, you don't notice the extra pounds. I look at that husband and think, *He did well.*

"If she puts some effort into her appearance and is comfortable in her own skin, you don't notice the extra pounds. I look at that husband and think, *He did well.*"

WHERE DO I START?

If you're pretty sure this chapter was meant for you, but you want to run it by your husband first, my recommendation is simple and heartfelt:

Don't.

Most men are wincingly sensitive about this subject, mostly because they remember how wincingly sensitive *we've* been on it in the past. Think about it—if your husband approached you about this, no matter how gently, what would you do? Probably the same as I have done in similar circumstances: burst into tears. That is enough to make most men so distressed and uncomfortable that they will never bring it up again. One man who had dipped his toe in those waters before said, "I know that if I bring it up, it will just hurt her feelings too much. So I'm going to preserve her feelings at the expense of my happiness, or satisfaction, or whatever you want to call it."

> Your man is not likely to be completely truthful, even if you—in all earnestness—want the truth.

Your man is not likely to be completely truthful, even if you—in all earnestness—want the truth. Consider, instead, applying Jeff's rule (my own husband to the rescue again). It's a self-inventory that's been confirmed by pretty much every other guy I've spoken with. Jeff's rule is this: if you are not realistically happy with your overall appearance and fitness level, assume he's not either.

Don't make him tell you that—both for your sake and the sake of your future together. (And for the sake of your sanity, note the important words *realistically* and *overall*. We're not talking about someone who is fit and trim but thinks she needs to lose five pounds or is dissatisfied with a certain feature. And we're *certainly* not talking about someone who takes care of herself and eats right but just has a body type that is completely different from the ballet dancer next door.)

A man gets very frustrated when the woman in his life endlessly anguishes about her appearance but takes little or no meaningful action. Many of the comments on the survey echoed what one man wrote: "If she wants to look better, she needs to do something about it, not just complain about it all the time."

At this point, some of you may be throwing your hands up in despair. Even if effort is really what matters, how, you wonder, are you supposed to add this effort to your many others?

Well, once you decide to take action, some very good news opens up to you. As it turns out, the person who cares so deeply about you taking care of yourself is, in almost every case, ready to be part of the solution.

Good News, Part 1: Your Man Wants to Help You

Almost every man I talked with said he would do whatever it takes to help his partner make this particular effort. And that was overwhelmingly confirmed by the follow-up survey.

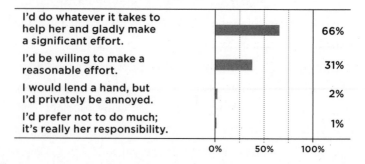

Imagine your wife/significant other is overweight and really wants to make the effort to get in shape, for you. But her slate is already full; she has no time during the day, and in the evening she has to watch the kids or drive them to their activities. How much effort, financial expense, or additional responsibility would you be willing to take on so she can do what's necessary to get in shape? (Choose one answer.)

I'd do whatever it takes to help her and gladly make a significant effort.	66%
I'd be willing to make a reasonable effort.	31%
I would lend a hand, but I'd privately be annoyed.	2%
I'd prefer not to do much; it's really her responsibility.	1%

Only four men out of four hundred said they'd be unwilling to help, and it's highly unlikely that your man is one of those cads—er, unaccommodating husbands. Almost everyone else (97 percent) said they would help willingly. One interviewee told me, "If a guy's wife suddenly verbalizes that she's determined to drop some weight and needs his help, any guy is going to jump to it! 'What can I do? Here's a credit card!'"

My husband drew a youthful comparison. "Look," he said, "when we were teenagers, the guys were always busy playing football or whatever. But if our girlfriends needed a ride to the tanning salon, we'd drop everything and drive them in a heartbeat. We'd even give them money to go! It was in our best interest! And that feeling doesn't change as we get older—we're willing to help our wives."

Maybe he watches the kids in the evening or drives the soccer carpool so you have time to work out. Maybe he stops bringing a particularly dangerous food into the house. Maybe he cooks dinner so you don't have to prepare foods you're trying to avoid. Or maybe he agrees to go on the diet with you. (Jeff has sheepishly admitted that several diets he has tried were—at their core—veiled attempts to get me to join him!)

And remember, since it's your sincere concern and effort that matters most, you can expect to see relationship benefits coming your way very soon.

Good News, Part 2: There's a Revolution in the Resources to Help You

Over the years I've tried almost every diet under the sun, only to watch helplessly as the weight crept back. (Can you relate?) But now I've learned that almost everything I had known about healthful eating was wrong. No wonder nothing worked long term! But there has now been a revolution in our scientific understanding of what eating well actually means (for example, eating good carbs and good fats and avoiding bad ones).

Without that knowledge, it is likely that we will keep sabotaging our efforts over the long term. Thankfully, several well-respected books are now available on what it really means to eat well and thus maintain a lifelong healthy weight. (On a personal note, I feel like I can stick with my new eating habits for the rest of my life because of the education I gained from *The South Beach Diet* by cardiologist Dr. Arthur Agatston.)

Good News, Part 3: God Will Help You

You probably feel battered by all of this information, so let me encourage you: God will help you address this health and fitness issue in amazing ways once you realize you need to.

Now that my eyes have been opened to the fact that my efforts are actually so important to my husband (and, conversely, that my lack of effort is so hurtful), you wouldn't believe the difference it has made in my motivation. I feel like the Lord has blessed my desire to serve my husband and our marriage by giving me a permanent internal motivation to have a healthy "temple." And I know He will do the same for you.

> God will help you address this health and fitness issue in amazing ways once you realize you need to.

I hope you have read this chapter prayerfully, allowing God to give you peace rather than a knot in your stomach. God is a God of peace, after all. And He—like our husbands—loves us no matter what our imperfections are.

Ten

WORDS FOR YOUR HEART

What Your Man Most Wishes You Knew About Him

*The one thing men most wish
they could tell us...*

We've come almost to the end of our journey together. But before I get to the final, most important revelation about the inner lives of men, I want to offer something from my heart as I walk this path with you.

Some of us may be challenged by what we have learned in these pages. These realities may not fit our idealistic or politically correct views of men. But just as we have discussed the difficult choices we expect our men to make, we must make our own. We can remain behind our safe, carefully constructed viewpoints about our men, or we can step out in courage to face the truth—and all that it means for what we must become.

Let us accept this call to maturity.

Let us accept this call to maturity and receive this invitation for our generation to become the strong, gentle, godly women our men need. If we are willing to be molded by His hands, the Lord will shower us, our men, and our relationships with abundance. That is the way He works. He made us for each other. He is the Author of love.

And that brings me to the conclusion of our journey—the single most important thing you need to know about the inner lives of men. The response that surprised me the most from the survey.

THE NUMBER-ONE SURVEY RESPONSE

As you now know, I asked the survey respondents one open-ended question that they could answer however they wanted:

What is the one thing that you wish your wife/significant other knew, but you feel you can't explain to her or tell her?

Hundreds of responses rolled in, and far and away the top response was this:

How much I love her.

I was stunned. Here was a perfect opportunity for men to vent, if they wanted to, or to share those things they wished their mates would work on. And yet, by far, the largest number of those responding—almost twice as many as the next highest response—chose to use the space to say that they wished their wives knew how much they loved them (or the cousin statement, that there was nothing they couldn't share because they had a great relationship).

After I shared this truth at a large community group, a man came down front after the talk and told me, "That is so true. And it's not that I don't tell my wife that I love her! I tell her that all the time. It's that I never seem to be able to tell her in a way that she'll believe me."

One man surveyed seemed to perfectly capture the way many men feel about the women in their lives, even if there are things in the relationship that need work. He answered that he wished his wife knew, "How important some things are to me that I won't mention because she's more important to me than all those other things."

Men want to show us how much they love us, and they also

long for their women to understand what is going on inside even though they sometimes can't explain it well. In the years since the original edition of this book came out, one of the most powerful things I have seen is the men whose eyes tear up as they listen to me explain these truths, moved by the thought that their wives might be able to—or want to—truly understand them.

So in the Interest of Understanding... the Top Five

In earlier pages, you saw the responses to each of the multiple-choice survey questions. But when the men wrote in what was most important to them, out of all the primary topics, the top five responses looked like this. In reverse order:

10%   "I need her to understand my burden to provide / how draining my job is."

10%   "I need more sex."

15%   "I need more respect, in private and public."

18%   "I wish she'd make more of an effort to take care of herself."

And number one...

32%   "I want her to know how much I love her" / "There's nothing I can't tell her."

Out of the infinite number of topics a man could mention, to have so many men say that one same thing is astounding...and wonderful.

"HOW MUCH I LOVE HER"

I'll close by reprinting here a sample of the loving comments from the survey. We've talked a lot in this book about all those things your man may need but intentionally haven't dealt with what you and I need. What we need, of course, is to feel our men's love. And if your man is like most men, he really does long to show it to you.

"The One Thing I Most Wish My Wife Knew..." (in Alphabetical Order)

- "After so many years, I hope my wife knows that she is the best hope in my life. We don't have everything that we desire material-wise, but there is so much more to life than that. I hope my wife knows that I love her and cherish our friendship, forever."
- "How great of a person I think she is."
- "How happy she makes me even when I am stressed or down about something else."
- "How much I love and appreciate her."
- "How much I love her."
- "How much I really care."
- "How much I truly do care for and love her and the kids."
- "How much she means to me."

- "I am very happy with my wife…. She may not be the perfect woman, but she is the perfect woman for me."
- "I have a perfect wife and marriage!"
- "I have a wonderful relationship with my wife and we communicate well. I wouldn't change a thing."
- "I love her and only her. It doesn't matter that our relationship isn't perfect—my love for her is so deep that nothing could break it."
- "I love my wife and want to be with her."
- "I love you. Please understand me. Make the leap to try."
- "I love you with all my heart."

"I love her with all my heart and would do anything it took to keep that love alive."

- "I wish that she knew how much I look up to her for *all* she is—intelligent, beautiful, capable, sexy, creative, generous, and kind. It seems that not a day passes when she doesn't feel insecure in one of these categories (or sometimes more than one). I wish that she had the confidence in herself that I have in her."

- "I would like her to know every day that I love her with all my heart and would do anything it took to keep that love alive."
- "That I am a sensitive man who loves deeply and wants to be loved deeply. And that I want to serve her if she would just let me."
- "That I love her more than she thinks I do."
- "That I will love her no matter what."
- "That she is the most important thing in life."
- "That she truly is the light of my life."
- "We have been together a long time, and I hope she knows I will always love her."

THE HOPE OF ORDINARY MEN

As you have read these insights into the inner lives of men, I hope you walk away with two main realizations: How much our men love us. And how much power God has given us to either tear them down or build them up to be the men He created them to be.

One Sunday morning, as we were concluding a pastoral interview in front of his congregation, a well-known pastor said something that perfectly captured this—and took my breath away. He stood up from where we had been sitting, walked to the front of the stage, and gazed out upon a vast auditorium of thousands. His voice was quiet with emotion: "I know you all think you have a good pastor. You don't. *You have a great pastor's wife.*" He knew what all men know, and what we now have the opportunity to do something about, every day, from now on.

Let me close with this great encouragement one man provided for every woman out there who wants to support her man in becoming all God intends him to be.

> It is so true that behind every great man is a great woman. There are a lot of men out there who are mediocre simply because their wives will not support them and bring them to greatness. And there are a lot of mediocre men who are destined to become great men—who *are becoming* great men—because their wives love and support them.
>
> My wife expects great things from me, even though I'm a pretty ordinary guy, really. She looks at me like I'm a genius in my field. She respects me in public and affirms me in private. I love her. And like all men, I want to live up to her expectations.

May the truths you've encountered here and in the preceding chapters encourage you to go forward in your new understanding of your man with hope, in confidence, and in peace.

Acknowledgments

Both editions of this book required the help and input of hundreds of people, and although I cannot list them all here, they have my deepest thanks. A few, however, *must* be mentioned.

The professional surveys that form the backbone of this book were guided and directed by Chuck Cowan of Analytic Focus (analyticfocus.com) and performed by the excellent team at Decision Analyst (decisionanalyst.com).

I am so grateful for the honesty and vulnerability of the many men who were willing to be interviewed, and to protect their privacy, I will not list them here. But I would like to thank Dr. Emerson Eggerichs of Love and Respect Ministries (loveandrespect.com), Daniel Weiss of Focus on the Family, Ken Ruettgers, and the other men listed by name in the book for their willingness to share their insight.

If this book is anointed by the Father in any way, it is because a dedicated team prayed for it every day—in fact, two different teams for the two different editions. They know that they did the real work of prayer, and I am so very, very grateful.

Most important, God used a small team of people—mostly men—to actively shape this book. My eternal gratitude goes to these core advisors: my husband, Jeff (I'll get back to him in a minute); my book agent, Calvin Edwards; and my world-class editors, Dave and Heather Kopp, as well as Bill Jensen and Don Jacobson at the original Multnomah. I'm so very grateful for my continuing partnership with Dave and the rest of the team at WaterBrook Multnomah, including Steve Cobb, Ken Petersen, Carie Freimuth, and Alison O'Hara, as well as for the editing aid of Amy McDonell, Eric Stanford, and Laura Wright on this revision.

Also important were my parents, Dick and Judy Reidinger, my brother, Rick, and my team of male and female readers, including Lisa and Eric Rice, D. J. Snell, Nancy French, Dan Maljanian, Jim Sharp, Roger Scarlett, Ann Browne, Katie Gates, Alison Darrell, Julie Anne Fidler, Bruce and Sue Osterink, and many others. Jenny Reynolds was deeply important as my research assistant on every aspect of the brain science, for this book and others.

Starting when *For Women Only* was first published in 2004, God used the explosion of interest in this book to raise up a whole ministry dedicated to equipping people to thrive in life and relationships through research and eyeopening truths. And in the last eight years, I could not have done *any* of it—or written this new edition—without the incredible support of my staff team, especially Linda Crews, my amazing director of operations who has built the ministry with me, and the outreach support of my wonderful speaking agent, Naomi Duncan. Throughout 2012, Linda and my staff members, Cathy Kidd, Karen Newby, Sally Hendry, and Theresa Colquitt, helped to take everything else off my plate so I could write this new edition and work on other books.

Finally, there is no way to adequately express my love and respect to my husband, Jeff. Bud, there is no other person as responsible for the content of *any* of my books as you. God has given you a special gift of insight and the ability to put into words so many things you would otherwise have found difficult to articulate. Your partnership on these projects has been one of the great joys of my life, and your wisdom, prayer, encouragement, and steadfast support have meant more than I can ever say. You are an example of what a husband should be, which is why my greatest gratitude goes to the Author of love, who gave us to each other.

Notes

1. *The Natural,* directed by Barry Levinson, TriStar Pictures, 1984.
2. "Attached," episode 160 of *Star Trek: The Next Generation,* originally aired November 8, 1993.
3. Francis X. Maguire, *You're the Greatest! How Validated Employees Can Impact Your Bottom Line,* ed. Steve Williford (Germantown, TN: Saltillo, 2001), 210–11.
4. Jack Welch and John A. Byrne, *Jack: Straight from the Gut* (New York: Warner, 2001), 5.
5. Many of the brain-science details in this chapter are drawn from Michael Gurian, *What Could He Be Thinking? How a Man's Mind Really Works* (New York: Macmillan, 2004).
6. Gurian, *What Could He Be Thinking?* 86, emphasis mine.
7. *The Lord of the Rings: The Return of the King,* directed by Peter Jackson, New Line Cinema, 2003.
8. Charlie Rich, "Behind Closed Doors," *Behind Closed Doors,* copyright © 1973, Epic Records.
9. Jill Eggleton Brett, "Not Tonight, Dear…," *Today's Christian Woman,* March/April 2002, 68.
10. Beyond the information in this chapter, further details and detailed citations on the male visual brain wiring can be found on pages 250–53 and 320 of my book *The Male Factor.* But here are a few starting points. One good study about the visual

brain wiring and the action of the nucleus accumbens was conducted by a group of scientists from Massachusetts General Hospital, Harvard Medical School, and Massachusetts Institute of Technology using functional MRI scans. Itzhak Aharon et al., "Beautiful Faces Have Variable Reward Value: fMRI and Behavioral Evidence," *Neuron* 32, no. 3 (November 2001): 537–51. Another study, by Emory University researchers, shows that when men and women see stimuli they perceive as sexual, most men have stronger biological responses than most women. Stephan Hamann et al., "Men and Women Differ in Amygdala Response to Visual Sexual Stimuli," *Nature Neuroscience* 7, no. 4 (April 2004): 411–16. And Joseph LeDoux, a neuroscientist at the Center for Neural Science at New York University, was the first to identify the "shortcut" for gut-level memories that can bypass the thinking centers of the brain and pop up again. Joseph LeDoux, "Emotional Memory Systems in the Brain," *Behavioural Brain Research* 58, nos. 1–2 (December 20, 1993): 69–79; "Emotion, Memory, and the Brain," *Scientific American* 270 (June 1994): 50–57; "Emotion and the Limbic System Concept," *Concepts in Neuroscience* 2 (1991): 169–99.

11. Stephen Arterburn and Fred Stoeker, *Every Man's Battle: Winning the War on Sexual Temptation One Victory at a Time* (Colorado Springs: WaterBrook, 2009).

12. *When Harry Met Sally,* directed by Rob Reiner, MGM Studios, 1989.

Dig deeper!

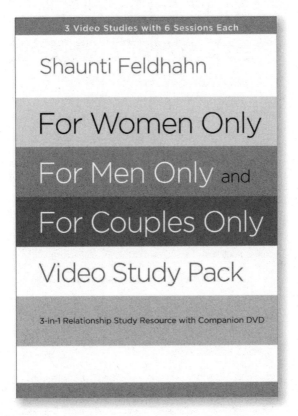

3 Video Studies with 6 Sessions Each

Shaunti Feldhahn

For Women Only

For Men Only and

For Couples Only

Video Study Pack

3-in-1 Relationship Study Resource with Companion DVD

Ideal for individuals or small groups, the *For Women Only, For Men Only and For Couples Only Video Study Pack* offers materials for women, for men, and for couples. This resource with DVDs and a participant's guide, fosters thoughtful inter-action, enabling couples to communicate better and embrace each other's differences.

Finally.
You Can Understand Her

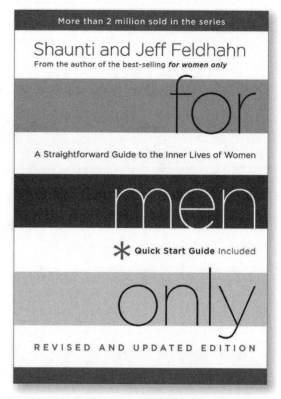

What makes her tick? What is she really asking (but not actually saying)? Take the guesswork out of trying to please your wife or girlfriend and begin loving her in the way she needs. Easily. *For Men Only* is a straightforward map that will lead you straight into her heart.

Read an excerpt from this book and more at
www.WaterBrookMultnomah.com

Also available from Shaunti!

Read excerpts from these books and more at
www.WaterBrookMultnomah.com

Shaunti Feldhahn Showed You How Men Think At Home —Now Find Out What They Think At Work

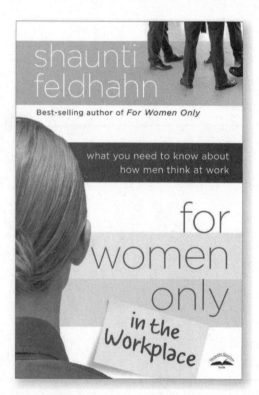

Do you know the unwritten rules of the workplace? *For Women Only in the Workplace* will equip you to be an effective Christian business-woman no matter what your circumstances.